JAPAN
and Its World

The 1975 Brown & Haley Lectures are the twenty-second of a series that has been given annually at the University of Puget Sound, Tacoma, Washington, by a scholar distinguished for work in the Social Studies or Humanities. The purpose of these lectures is to present original analyses of some intellectual problems confronting the present age.

JAPAN

and Its World

Two Centuries
of Change

Marius B. Jansen

Princeton University Press
Princeton, New Jersey

Published by Princeton University Press,
41 William Street, Princeton, New Jersey 08540
In the United Kingdom by Princeton University Press,
Chichester, West Sussex
Copyright © 1980 by Princeton University Press;
preface to the paperback edition © 1995
by Princeton University Press
All Rights Reserved

Publication of this book has been aided by the Whitney
Darrow Publication Reserve Fund of Princeton
University Press

Library of Congress Cataloging-in-Publication Data

Jansen, Marius B.
  Japan and its world.
  (The Brown and Haley lectures, 1975)
  Bibliography: p.
  Includes index.
  1. Japan—Addresses, essays, lectures. I. Title.
II. Series: Brown & Haley lectures; 1975.
DS806.J16   952   80-7532
ISBN 0-691-05310-3 (cloth)
ISBN 0-691-00640-7 (paperback)

Princeton University Press books are printed on acid-free
paper and meet the guidelines for permanence and
durability of the Committee on Production Guidelines
for Book Longevity of the Council on Library Resources

First Princeton Paperback printing, 1995
Printed in the United States of America
by Princeton Academic Press

10 9 8 7 6 5 4 3 2

for Fred and Dottie Haley

FOREWORD

Often during the twenty-five years since the establishment of the Brown & Haley lectures, I had felt that the time would come when the lectureship committee would wish to have the lectures delivered by my friend Marius Jansen.

But Marius was also a close friend of the late Professor Lyle S. (Stan) Shelmidine, history professor at the University of Puget Sound, who, with my father and me, was instrumental in setting up the lectureship and was its committee chairman until his death in 1966.

It is with especial pride therefore that I see these lectures appear in their usual slim volume, and should like to add that they embody perfectly the initial criteria which we set up when the lectureship was first established: (1) that the lectures be done "by an outstanding scholar in the field of the social studies or humanities"; (2) that the lectures "relate . . . in a palpable manner to urgent problems confronting society today"; and, since publication was to be a part of the plan, (3) that they contain new, unpublished material and therefore add usefully to the sum of knowledge.

June 10, 1976

Fred T. Haley, President
Brown & Haley

CONTENTS

LIST OF ILLUSTRATIONS

PREFACE TO THE 1995
PAPERBACK EDITION

It is now two decades since these lectures were given at the University of Puget Sound in Tacoma, Washington. The United States Bicentennial commemoration, which furnished my initial point of departure, is well behind us. In 1995, Japanese face very different anniversaries. The first is the inception of empire with the success of Japan's first modern war through victory over Imperial China. In 1895 the Treaty of Shimonoseki was the first step in Japan's effort to join the great Western powers of its day. More fateful by far, of course, and much larger in the consciousness of contemporary Japanese, is the commemoration of defeat in 1945. A half century of militarism, war, and emperor-centered nationalism has now been followed by as many years of peace under a constitution that describes the emperor as "symbol" of the state and asserts the sovereignty of the people. The Emperor Hirohito, known posthumously as Shōwa for the sixty-two-year era of his reign, died in 1989, and Japanese have been looking back as well as forward.

At just this juncture the world to which postwar Japanese have accommodated themselves has been in process of rapid change. The sudden disintegration of the Soviet Union ended the bipolar structure of international power that had prevailed since 1945. As a consequence the United States has begun to give economic concerns a priority that had been denied so long as security relations with Japan came first. Nor is Japan's economic growth an isolated "miracle" in Asia any longer. All along the maritime fringe of Asia the Republic of Korea, the Republic of China on Taiwan, Hong Kong, and Singapore have achieved impressive growth rates that are now beginning to impact on Thailand, Malaysia, Indonesia, and other Southeast Asian states. At the century's end Asia is registering the fastest growth rates in the world. In turn the People's Republic of China, though resisting political liberalization, has relaxed its economic controls, welcomed foreign capital, and taken important strides toward becoming what some predict will be the largest economy in the world. In China's coastal provinces trade and factories grow apace, and new chimneys pour acid rain on Japanese forests.

The United States too has changed. It is now the only superpower, but its relative strength and leverage are much reduced from what they were in postwar decades. During the 1980s staggering budget deficits made America the world's largest debtor nation, while Japan emerged as the largest creditor. The yen rose steadily in value as the dollar plunged. Japanese overseas investment burgeoned, especially in Asia but also in the United States, and as wages in Japan increased Japanese enterprises moved offshore in search of cheaper labor and the security of markets from which they could not be excluded. Meanwhile purchases of highly visible parcels of United States real estate produced negative reactions that startled many Japanese.

The Gulf War of 1991 showed that rogue dictators were no longer able to exploit superpower rivalry. It underscored other changes as well. Military muscle was provided by American weapons whose technological sophistication was flashed around the world by United States media, but Japan's provision of 13 billion dollars was the largest contribution after that of Saudi Arabia. Japan was emerging as the world's banker, but without much appreciation. The Tokyo government's awkward handling of its contribution brought journalistic criticism of "checkbook diplomacy."

The end of the Cold War had equally important results in Japanese politics. The ruling Liberal-Democratic party, which had been in power since its formation in 1956, was weakened by a series of scandals that jeopardized its legitimacy and brought demands for change. Breakaway members formed new splinter parties that united with the socialist opposition to form a series of short-lived and unstable governments. The first of these, under a popular governor of Kumamoto, was able to secure changes in electoral laws designed to bring government closer to the people. No one could be confident of their effect, but it seemed clear that a political order long mired in inertia was finally showing signs of change. Ideology changed with politics and world affairs. In 1994 Japan's socialists renounced most of the positions they had affirmed for decades to join a coalition government with their erstwhile opponents of the Liberal Democratic Party. On every hand politicians called for more responsive government, but at the same time the bureaucracy, its position strengthened by the political instability around it, showed little interest in loosening the regulatory powers that were its strength. Despite announcements that Japan had reached a turning point, consequently, the ship of state seemed unlikely to turn quickly. Deeply entrenched interests and attitudes in business, bureaucracy, and government combine to guarantee that change will be incremental and gradual.

The same is true of attitudes. Japan's economic clout has made it a major player in every international organization, but those organizations have yet to acknowledge this by structural change. United Nations achievements in resolving the Cambodian political impasse and in dealing with unprecedented waves of refugees in Africa and Southeast Asia were directed by Japanese officials of that body. In response to calls for larger-scale participation, the Japanese Diet reluctantly and cautiously authorized a small Peace Keeping Organization that marked the first dispatch of Japanese participants overseas since World War II. Intense Diet debate resulted in limitations that kept them unarmed to avoid the possibility of participation in violence, however, and served to remind observers of the distaste most Japanese felt for any revival of "great power" ambitions. A few political leaders, on the other hand, began to argue that it was time for Japan to resume the stance of a "normal country" by altering its constitutional ban on armaments to bring it into line with twenty-first-century realities. Debates suppressed for fifty years were once again becoming possible.

In all of this, Japanese began to show a new and stronger Asian consciousness, one so striking that some spoke of an "Asianization" of Japan. It could hardly have been otherwise. In 1985 Japan traded a third more with the United States than it did with Asia, but by 1993 the reverse was true: Japan's trade with Asia was a third larger than that with the United States. Burgeoning Japanese off-shore investment in Asia contributed to Asian integration through cooperation with the Association of Southeast Asian States (ASEAN) and the Asian-Pacific Economic Cooperation (APEC). Japan became China's largest trading partner, and China was Japan's second largest. From 1981 to 1991 total world trade increased in real terms by 48 percent, but for Japan, and for the rest of East Asia, it doubled. In Japanese educational institutions students from Asia vastly outnumbered those from Western countries.

In short, since these lectures were given Japan's world has changed powerfully. In 1975 I spoke with astonishment of the more than three million Japanese who traveled overseas, but in 1994 that total rose to 13.5 million, four-fifths of them tourists. It is still far too early to select a successor to Sugita Gempaku, Kume Kunitake, and Matsumoto Shigeharu (who died in 1989), the three I used as examples twenty years ago. But it is reasonably certain that he or she will be more of a citizen of the world than those who went before.

It was originally R. Miriam Brokaw, then Associate Director and Editor of Princeton University Press, who urged me to submit these lectures to the Press for publication, and it is a pleasant duty to add this word of appreciation to her and to her successors who have suggested reissuing them once more.

Princeton, 1995   *M.B.J.*

JAPAN
and Its World

INTRODUCTION

The United States Bicentennial provided an inviting occasion to look back over the changes that have taken place in Japan during those centuries. Two hundred years ago Japan was a small, underdeveloped country, largely secluded from the outside world. A hundred years later, however, it had resolved to restructure its institutions on Western lines, and sent a good part of its governing elite on an extensive tour of the Western world to observe the sources of wealth and strength in other countries. For the Philadelphia Centennial Exposition of 1876 Japan sent an impressive exhibit surpassed by few in size and by none in interest as notice of the nation's intent to modernize and internationalize. The exhibit was of such quality that one writer confessed: "We have been accustomed to regard that country as uncivilized, or half-civilized at the best, but we found here abundant evidences that it outshines the most cultivated nations of Europe in arts which are their pride and glory, and which are regarded as among the proudest tokens of their high civilization."* Today, three decades after its crushing defeat in World War II Japan is one of the great powers in the world, and one of the small number of industrialized democracies.

* Quoted by Neil Harris, in "All the World a Melting Pot? Japan at American Fairs, 1876-1904," in Akira Iriye, ed. *Mutual Images: Essays in American-Japanese Relations* (Cambridge: Harvard University Press, 1975), p. 30.

It is little wonder that Japanese perceptions of the outside world have shifted sharply throughout these two centuries. The pages which follow focus on those perceptions. Japan's emergence from isolation to international importance was an event of central importance to world history and especially to the history of the United States. In the twentieth century the transition was blurred by misunderstanding and error on both sides and punctuated by violence. The United States, no less than Japan, was emerging into international importance during the same period, and its perceptions of international society underwent changes scarcely less dramatic than those of Japan.

No part of those perceptions shifted more erratically than American views of Japan. On the shelves of our libraries, books whose titles promise a friendly, beguiling, and exotic Japan rub shoulders with others that warn against an aggressive, angry, and suspicious rival. Since the war the danger of military attack has faded from this focus, only to reappear at times as warning of a hard-working, humorless, and desperately skillful economic competitor. The prognosticators have shifted slowly from emphasis upon a Japan destined for poverty without its mainland and colonial holdings, to a Japan that was after all going to survive through hard work and modest living, to a Japan that was surely going to take over the world through its burgeoning economic growth. Postwar titles mix optimism and even dismay about the new superpower with metaphors like blossoms to indicate its fragility. It is not to be wondered at that the Japanese themselves exhibit mercurial shifts from euphoria to depression.

The intellectual and psychological aspects of the Japanese world view have deeper historical roots than the speculations of journalists and pundits, however; and it is these aspects of Japanese history that have dominated much of my work for many years. They seem to me increasingly central to an understanding of modern Japan and of modern East Asia. Until recently the Japanese have seen their world as a hierarchy, and their tendency to rank the countries in it in order of esteem and importance undoubtedly owed much to the structure of their own society and experience. I have tried in these lectures to examine changes in that ranking through the careers and views of some particularly interesting figures. The flood of recent publications and commentary makes it particularly inviting to focus the discussion in this way. It is nevertheless a field in which our study of Japan is still at a very early stage, and it is my hope that these discussions will indicate to others some of the rewards and possibilities of this kind of inquiry.

The lectures stand as they were given, although some facts, statistics, and titles have been added to make allowance for recent developments and publication.

Citations, with one or two exceptions, have been placed in the Bibliographical Note.

Princeton, 1979   *M.B.J.*

I

Challenges to the Confucian Order in the 1770's

Anyone who titles a set of lectures "Japan's Bicentennial" has to begin by explaining what it is that he proposes to commemorate. Our own Bicentennial at the moment needs no defense, for the importance of 1776 is clear. A few years ago the Japanese were busy with a Centennial of their own, but in the Meiji Restoration of 1868 they too had a clearly distinguishable event. I have nothing so sharply etched for the 1770's in Japan. What I do have to discuss is the beginnings of decisive change in the way the Japanese perceived their world. Changes of this sort are not usually associated with a single great event. They are rather the fruit of a series of events in thought and in publication that prepare the way for the political events to come.

I have rather good company in claiming great importance for the 1770's. Some years ago Donald Keene wrote of men in this period that "one has entered a new age, that of modern Japan. One finds . . .

a new spirit, restless, curious, and receptive." And, more recently, the Tokyo University historian Haga Tōru* has written that "in the mid 1770's the Japanese experienced changes in consciousness, in their way of thinking and in perception, to an altogether profound degree." The products of this included publication of a work on electricity, and another expressing pointed preference for Western approaches to physics over the explanations in traditional Chinese learning. But the shift is probably most appropriately symbolized by the celebrated decision of the doctor Sugita Gempaku to be present at the dissection of an executed criminal in 1771. "Old Mother Green Tea," the subject of the inquiry, proved through the arrangement of her viscera that a Dutch book on anatomy that Sugita had acquired was correct and that textbooks of Chinese medicine were wrong. It was not true, as some had explained, that Westerners and Orientals were constructed differently. Or, as had also been suggested, that rigor mortis resulted in a rearrangement of the body's parts. Sugita and his companion resolved, as they walked home, to translate the work; "and we made a vow," he wrote later, "to seek facts through experiment." In 1774 they published the volume in question, thereby beginning an age of translation of Western books into Japanese. The very next year Sugita, in a dialogue he entitled "Words of a Crazy Doctor," cheerfully took on the whole Chinese cultural tradition.

This event was of profound significance for Japan's

* Japanese names are given in the Japanese order, with surname first.

world view. The steps in question served as symbols, but also as agents, for the demolition of a traditional view of the outside world.

In order to show why this was so, and what it was that changed, it is necessary to begin with some comments on that traditional view, and particularly with consideration of the ties that had for so long bound Japan to China.

1. *The Chinese Colossus*

It is a truism to observe that Japan was in the Chinese cultural orbit. China was the source for Japan's writing system, its cultural values in literature, philosophy, and thought, and its institutional examples in government and law. Chinese civilization flowed into a less developed and less coherent Japan to affect the formulation of its culture at a very early point. China was also the channel for the religious values and sectarian developments of Buddhism. The origin was Indian, but the expression and organization were Chinese. The Japanese debt to the Chinese cultural order was thus very great, and perhaps unique. It is true that many scholars, among them E. O. Reischauer, would hold that Japan's debt to its neighbors is not really greater than that of other countries. Every country borrows, he has argued, and we do wrong to isolate and emphasize the Japanese case. It is also true that recent advances in our understanding of prehistoric Japan help to put this borrowing in better perspective. There was more to prehistoric Japan than we thought; the land bridge to the mainland in prehistoric times permitted far more movement than can be documented. Japan was a participant in, and not merely a recipient of, early civilization. Carbon dating has moved back the borders of early civilization in the Japanese islands to give Japan the world's oldest pottery culture, for instance, with a continuous development from remote antiquity. In historic times, Chinese influence was never so great that it ruled out Japanese selectivity and modification in the cultural and institutional borrowing that took place. The most basic social and cultural values remained distinct.

Despite all this, I think the Japan-China relationship was clearly unique in its intimacy and longevity. It was so for a number of reasons, some of which apply to Japan, and more to China. I would give six elements that combined to make it so.

The first was the insularity and isolation of Japan. Japan was farther from its sources of outside influence, and more remote, than was true of any other major country. The Tsushima straits are sometimes compared to those of Dover, but to compare them is to emphasize the contrast. Ocean winds and currents, geography and distance, all worked together to leave Japan isolated unless there was sustained purpose in making the contact. I do not think anyone has ever swum to Korea. In the sixteenth century the Portuguese came to Japan by accident, blown off course. Japan's insularity made its people more conscious of the China tie, and more aware of the import. *Karamono*, things from China, were distinct and easily labelled; so, by extension, was *karagokoro*, the

"Chinese spirit" that the eighteenth-century scholar Motoori deplored. So too with medicine, painting, poetry, and prose; *kanpō*, *kanga*, *kanshi*, *kanbun*, and many other things that could be set off from the native as "Chinese."

In the second place, China was the only external influence into modern times. Korea was there, of course, and served as channel for a great deal, but almost always as vessel for Chinese contents. The awareness of India came with Buddhism, but India was out of reach until modern times and Buddhism came in Chinese translation. The options were limited, in other words; in early times it was China or nothing. Japan was on the periphery of one cultural sphere, and there was nothing on the other side.

Third was the enduring nature of the Chinese model. Unlike Palestine, Greece, and Rome, which influenced modern Europe, China continued present and powerful. For Japan, it served as a classical antiquity, a Renaissance Italy, and an eighteenth-century France all in one. It was a single cultural colossus, one that endured. England might lay claim to the greatness of Rome, and Russia to the heritage of the Byzantium that had fallen, but the living China always had prior claim to the heritage of the Chinese past.

Fourth, China provided a very special sort of model; it made no particular effort to sell itself, for it had no need to do so. Since China was so nonassertive, it may have been easier for the Japanese to be selective in their borrowing. But whatever effort was made had to come from Japan. And, since the path was long, often dangerous, and always expensive, the effort required organization and determination. The single attempt at invasion from China in the thirteenth century was not Chinese, but Mongol. In Mongol times, Buddhist abbots travelled to Japan to bring the teachings of Zen, and, in early Manchu years, a number of Confucian scholars made their way to Japan. But these visits were the products of desperately unsettled times, for Mongol and Manchu rule were aberrations in the Chinese pattern. The more usual Chinese attitude, from the founding emperor of the Ming to Chinese leaders of more recent times, has been to mix complaints about Japanese actions with indifference to Japanese culture.

Fifth, the contact was episodic. It was prompted by Japanese leadership only during periods of need, and the lull that followed invariably saw a surge of strongly Japanese cultural development. Several centuries of intensive effort from the seventh to the ninth were followed by a slow-down; mercantile and temple contacts in medieval times broke off again in the fourteenth century; official missions in the fifteenth and sixteenth centuries came to an end with the Manchu victory of 1644, and small-scale merchant contact was all that remained from then to modern times. Thus, occasional and intensive import resonated with a resurgence of the native cultural tradition to define a "Japan" as well as a "China." It is fitting that the first document written in borrowed Chinese characters was the Japanese mythology, with its statements of imperial divinity, and that one of the first compounds formed with Chinese readings was *Shintō*. Thus

China helped to define Japan. Gradually, however, isolation also made possible adaptation and assimilation, until "Japanese spirit"—*wakon*—could include much that was Chinese, so that modern Shintō carried a debt to Lao Tzu and to Taoism.

Sixth and last, the Chinese definitions of Chineseness in cultural rather than in geographical or racial terms—the universality of China's cultural values—made it possible for Japanese intellectuals to realize an unusually full membership in the Chinese cultural order. One is struck by the degree to which readers of popular novels in even twentieth-century Japan have been expected to recognize a wealth of allusions to Chinese poetry, history, and prose. Even without a common language, the Japanese and Chinese have been able to communicate by writing, jotting down characters and passing them back and forth. This exchange is weakening now, but as recently as 1972 Prime Minister Tanaka mustered up the courage to present Mao Tse-tung with a poem, allegedly his own, and found himself rewarded with a gift volume of the poems of Ch'u Yüan.

All this adds up to a very special relationship indeed, and some disclaimers that have to be added make that relationship even more distinctive by indicating the ambivalence with which the Japanese have usually regarded China. Japan was in the Chinese cultural orbit, but Japanese preferences in religion, verse, and art retained indigenous alternatives to the Chinese imports. In governmental and institutional patterns the Chinese models were soon modified beyond recognition.

Japan was never in the Chinese political orbit. Japanese leaders were never willing to accept the satellite status that China expected of its near neighbors. Official correspondence between the two countries began in the seventh century with Japanese messages so jaunty in tone that the Sui court of China took them to indicate inadequate cultural preparation. (That, incidentally, was also true of the first American message to the Ch'ing emperor twelve centuries later; it was couched in language that had been perfected for communications with Indian chiefs.) The literature about Japanese emissaries to the Chinese court is replete with celebrated instances of their courage (augmented by occasional recourse to magic) in overcoming supercilious Chinese under unpleasant and occasionally hazardous conditions. The T'ang Dynasty poet Po Chü-i was enormously popular in Japan. He long provided a model for Japanese poets who wrote in Chinese, and yet even he serves to illustrate the ambivalence of cultural attraction and the defensiveness which Japanese felt for China. A fifteenth-century Nō play named for him has as plot his appearance in Japan as symbol of an attempted conquest of Japanese civilization. Instead of meeting a docile race of imitators, however, he encounters an old fisherman who assures him that, unlike the case in China, where poetry is the plaything of the elite, in Japan poetry is a universal form of expression. Then, in a concluding dance, the fisherman, now revealed as Sumiyoshi, the god of (Japanese) poetry, produces by the action of his sleeves a breeze sufficient to drive the visitor's ship back to China.

The religious role of the Japanese emperor, who had special ties to the Shintō shrines and deities, probably operated to guarantee that Japan would never submit to the subservience required for ritual investment of the sort that China expected of its tributary states. Except for a brief aberration on the part of fifteenth-century shoguns, Japanese leaders never addressed the court of China in the way that it considered proper. Instead, when the sixteenth-century conqueror Hideyoshi reunited Japan, the proof of legitimacy he pursued—vainly—for himself was through conquest on the continent. Only in this way, perhaps, could he have established his independence from subordination to his own ruler without engendering a new dependency on the Ming emperor. Hideyoshi's plans and conquests were thwarted by the intervention of Ming armies on behalf of China's Korean tributary, however, and his own governance collapsed soon afterward.

2. China in Tokugawa Thought

All this is quite familiar. But my theme takes us to the 1770's, and this requires some comment on the seventeenth- and eighteenth-century setting within which the changes we shall consider took place.

In Japan the Tokugawa rulers came to power in 1600 and subdued their last major opponents in 1615. Unlike Hideyoshi, who pursued legitimacy through continental conquests, they concluded that their rule could best be safeguarded through a policy of seclusion—or, as a colleague of mine has phrased it, they chose voluntary solitary confinement for their country.

Tokugawa concerns were with stability and security. The century and more of feudal strife out of which the leaders had fashioned their victory had shown the possibilities for anarchy in unrestricted access to foreign goods and weapons. The spread of Japanese traders and settlers, some of them refugees from Japan's wars, throughout Southeast Asia offered the possibility of trade and perhaps even settlement there, but it also presented problems of control and of enrichment for possible rivals of the shogunate. Hideyoshi's Korean experience had demonstrated the practical difficulties involved in efforts at internationalism on Japanese terms. Internationalism remained possible on Chinese terms, but, although this was considered in the early years of Tokugawa rule, shogunal advisors seem to have concluded that there was no way of reconciling those terms with Japanese sovereignty and shogunal legitimacy. Minimizing trade, and controlling what remained, seemed the wiser course.

In the 1630's it became possible to assert the legitimacy of Tokugawa rule by closing the country to international trade. The ability of Catholic missionaries, who had first come a century before, to find converts among the feudality had shown the possibilities for subversion from abroad. The guns imported and then produced within Japan had speeded unification, but once the country was at peace they could only harm that peace and threaten the status and superiority symbolized by the swords of the samurai class. In 1637 a rebellion in southern Japan assumed Christian aspects. Feudal lords were summoned to put it down, and thereafter the proscription of Christianity could be ordered in every part of the country. Implementation of those orders provided the shogunate with an unparalleled device for interference in the affairs of each region of Japan.

Meanwhile the shogun renounced foreign interests in the Seclusion Edicts. "No Japanese ship," an edict warned, "may leave for foreign countries. No Japanese may go abroad secretly. If anybody tries to do this, he will be killed. . . . Any Japanese now living abroad who tries to return to Japan will be put to death. . . ." Vigorous persecution stamped out Japanese Christianity or drove it underground. Until the 1870's, notices in every village forbad the "religion of Jesus." Informers were rewarded, and compulsory registration with Buddhist temples provided a positive control for the negative bans on Christians.

The decision to forego international contacts was made easier by mighty events taking place in China, where the Manchus completed their conquest of the country in 1644. This inaugurated a period of great political strength. Chinese borders were expanded to the west and north as Manchu imperialism established the contours of modern China's sovereignty in regions never before under close Chinese rule. Within those borders dissidence was effectively suppressed. Along the Chinese coast, trade and regional autonomy seemed as threatening to Peking as did private trade to the shoguns across the water. It required half a century for the Manchus to control the southern coast, and Taiwan was captured only in 1683. Until that point, the coast was closed and even, for a time, evacuated. Japanese pirates and traders had been in frequent contact with the China coast for over two centuries before this time, and Chinese traders had been everywhere, but Tokugawa and Manchu power now broke that pattern. The shogunate saw the Manchu rise as a threat to East Asian stability. Not able to affect it, it chose to turn its back on the problem. The Manchu rulers did the same about Japan, and only a few Chinese traders from South China managed to maintain a small trade with Japan thereafter. They were housed and watched at Nagasaki, which also received a few Ming refugees.

By the eighteenth century, Japanese images of China and of the larger world were thus more complex than they had ever been before. Chinese books served as the medium for most classical learning, but China itself was under unfriendly and in fact "barbarian" rule. Chinese books were imported with Chinese goods by the traders who came to Nagasaki, including some concerned with science, but the books had to be cleared for infection by Christianity because they reflected the presence in China of Western missionaries who translated and taught Western science there until the eighteenth century. At Nagasaki the Protestant Dutch were permitted to trade after the Catholic Portuguese were banished, but they too were kept at arm's length lest they corrupt those near them. Both toward China and toward the West, in other words, emotions were more extreme and ambivalence more marked than ever before. This is an area still poorly studied, and it is one as difficult as it is fascinating for the historian.

Nevertheless, the harsh measures taken by the Tokugawa rulers succeeded in their object. Japan experienced over two centuries of peace and security. Those centuries of order encouraged the development of outlooks and of institutions that transformed the quarrelsome samurai of 1600 into a more responsible and more civilian-style bureaucracy, one that administered what became a permanent military government. The arts of peace and education flourished, and popular literacy and culture showed the permeation throughout Japanese society of values and learning that had previously been restricted to a small fraction of the elite.

One of the remarkable aspects of the Tokugawa years is that the Chinese literary heritage became more important than it had ever been. As a result, it was possible and in fact necessary for the Japanese to distinguish between "China" and Chinese culture. "China" as a country had fallen under Manchu rule, as centuries earlier it had fallen to the Mongols. This time, however, the awareness of that fact was far greater because changes within Japanese society had broadened the horizons of consciousness. Chinese books and Chinese refugees preserved the memory of the Manchu conquest long after censorship had dulled it within China itself.

On the other hand, Chinese civilization was never held in higher regard. The spread of education revived and deepened Japanese appreciation of the Confucian teachings. They became the main fare in schools for the elite, both those established by feudal authorities and the many private academies that flourished in the cities. In art the Kanō school peopled its landscapes with Chinese travellers and sages. An important group of amateur artists known as "the literati" styled themselves after the scholar-artists of late Ming times. There was an outpouring of poetry written in Chinese. And there was a tendency toward China worship. Many Confucian scholars wrote elegies in what they hoped was good Chinese, to express their distress at being restricted to the outer border of the Chinese culture zone. Ogyū Sorai, one of the most formidable of their number, at one point styled himself an "eastern barbarian living in Japan." Arai Hakuseki, a leading scholar-statesman of the early eighteenth century, balanced a jealous concern for the supremacy of his shogun with a personal eagerness for Chinese recognition and approval. He wanted the shogun to assume the title "King of Japan" in correspondence with Korea, and he instituted pseudo-archaic ceremonies to establish greater antiquity for his country, but he also did his best to get Ryūkyūan ambassadors to solicit an introductory note from a highly placed scholar in Peking for a volume of his Chinese poetry.

This was not the only position possible for the Confucianists. Some adopted the Chinese manner without its content, by claiming for Japan the benefits of "Central Country" and classifying China itself as border "barbarian." All who thought about it had to make some distinction between the Chinese ideal and Chinese history. The ideal was unquestioned and stood for civilization itself. China's history, however, was seriously flawed. Ogyū Sorai could espouse the classical tradition of the sages, even worshipfully so, while rejecting more recent trends of Confucian thought in China. He and his disciples observed that, while China had begun with feudalism and moved on to central imperial administration, Japan had gone in the reverse direction, from the classical regimes of the imperial past to the feudal divisions of their own day. Each, one could conclude, had its own validity. Arai Hakuseki did not hesitate to acknowledge Chinese literary tutelage, but he had no doubt about the political respect due Japan and its rulers. And Yamazaki Ansai, when asked by his students what their duty would be if Japan were threatened by an army captained by Confucius, told them to do as Confucius would have done, and resist.

The stream of Confucian learning was broad and it could accommodate many emphases. Toward the last, the shogunate did its best to limit varieties of interpretation and to encourage a single orthodoxy, but it lacked the setting of examination system and of imperial ideological primacy that made this feasible in China. Instead, shogun and feudal lords had recourse to the advice of scholars, who varied in their prescriptions for good government between the advocacy of fixed norms of behavior and allowance for an intuitive and inner morality. Each could be grounded in Chinese text and example, although the former was more congenial to bureaucratic hierarchy in Japan as it was in China. But, while Confucian learning was broad, and represented agreement on moral categories more than on details of dogma, those who carried that learning were not. The particularities of Japanese feudal hierarchy and a fastidious attention to status distinctions operated to favor punctilio in definition as they did in deportment, and often helped to produce a rigidity in belief as in action that helps to account for the relief with which later reformers sprang to attack the official learning as barren and "Chinese."

The ambivalence between cultural admiration— and even, at times, self-abasement—and political distance and even hostility that characterized Tokugawa attitudes toward China was not by any means new, for it had been shown by Japanese leaders and thinkers in earlier eras. What was probably new in the eighteenth century, however, was that this consciousness permeated down to popular culture as well, and that it proved an attractive theme there. Since at the popular level the cultural appreciation was more shallow and the cultural debt less conscious, a jaunty self-confidence seemed to predominate. Chikamatsu's famous drama *The Battles of Coxinga*, first performed in 1715 and a smash hit thereafter, celebrated the mighty deeds of a hero, offspring of a Chinese father and of a Japanese mother, who flourished on Taiwan between the fall of the Ming and the secure establishment of Manchu rule. Donald Keene's splendid translation provides evidence on a number of points. The playgoer's horizons were expected, despite the restrictions of the seclusion system, to extend well beyond Japan's borders. Coxinga's Japanese wife reproaches him that they had promised to go together, "not merely to China or Korea, but to India or to the ends of the clouds." The Japanese military tradition is praised. In launching the expedition against the Manchus, the narrator invokes the fourth-century Empress Jingū and her invasion of Korea. It is particularly interesting to find the Manchus denounced as despicable barbarians. The loyal Ming general contrasts a virtuous Ming with the barbarian Tartars. "This land which has given birth to the sages will soon fall under the yoke of Mongolia, and we shall become their slaves, differing from animals only in that we do not wag tails or have bodies covered with fur." His warning becomes fact: "The entire country . . . has been enslaved by the Tartar barbarians."

For this situation there is no solution but old-fashioned Japanese courage, and Coxinga's Japanese ancestry is exactly what is needed. He makes it clear that he, like his audience, is tired of being told he is from a small and insignificant land. "Vile creatures!" he shouts. "You who despise the Japanese for coming from a small country—have you learned now the meaning of Japanese prowess, before which even tigers tremble?" His secret weapon turns out to be his Japanese sword, whose "blade is imbued with the strength of the Japanese gods." It is so powerful, in fact, that Coxinga decides it would be unfair "to face a tiger with my sword." Still, something special is needed, and in the end a sacred charm from the Great Shrine at Ise exerts mysterious power to make the Chinese tiger droop its tail, hang its ears, and draw in its legs timidly. The narrator intones, "How awe-inspiring is the majestic power of the goddess Amaterasu!" Thus primitive small-nation chauvinism saves the day. In the climactic final battles at Nanking there is little doubt that the hero's victory is due "to the divine, the martial, and the saintly virtues of the emperor of Great Japan, a land endowed with perpetual blessings."*

It would be foolish to read too much into this extravaganza of stage entertainment, but the repetition in plebian form of so many of the themes that delighted the medieval aristocrats who studied scroll painting depicting the exploits of Ambassador Kibi no Mabiki in T'ang China cannot be entirely without its psychological significance. Clearly the Manchu conquest of China served to complicate Japanese attitudes further. Seventeeth-century writers had warned of a possible return of the Mongol danger, and as late as 1786 Hayashi Shihei tried to stir those fears, now dormant, by raising the suggestion that the Manchus, now that they had solved China's border problems by their conquests, might launch an invasion of Japan.

3. The Rejection of "China"

Until the eighteenth century the only serious alternative to Confucian philosophy was Buddhist. Since both of these schools had come by way of China, the primacy of Chinese learning had not been challenged by that contention. But by the late eighteenth century there were also Japanese thinkers prepared to reject the entire Chinese model, Confucian

* Donald Keene, tr., *The Battles of Coxinga* (London: Taylor's Foreign Press, 1951), also reprinted in *Major Plays of Chikamatsu* (New York: Columbia University Press, 1961).

as well as Buddhist. The most forthright of them were connected with the National Studies, or *kokugaku*, movement.

The eighteenth century witnessed tremendous development of literary and philosophical scholarship in Japan. Confucianists turned to the principal texts of their tradition with new rigor and determination in efforts to free those teachings from the accretions of subsequent interpretation. Specialists in Japanese poetry meanwhile developed their own enthusiasm for textual research. In the study of Japanese poetry they were dealing with the very center of Japanese aesthetics and values, and as they investigated the classics of Japanese antiquity they struggled to define what it was that lay at the center of the Japanese national character. In part this represented for them a psychological counter against the dominance of Confucianism and the influence of what seemed to them the formal, rule-centered scholarship of heavy-handed pedants. Like their counterparts and contemporaries, the German romantics, they looked for the free spirit of a native tradition, one that was in danger of being smothered under the borrowed standards and rigidity of foreign classicism.

The Japanese spirit, the national scholars proclaimed, was pure, natural, and unbounded, and the norms of Confucian morality were antithetical to it. Emotion was pure and honest, and to curb it through rules or to sublimate it through religion was dishonest. Such foreign deception and falsehood, Motoori wrote, were contrary to human nature. A proper awareness of the pathos of things was most clearly present in Japan's tradition of emotive poetry. Thus their path led back to the classics of the Japanese literary tradition and to values that could be discerned at the dawn of Japanese history before imports from China obscured their purity. The ancient cult of Shintō was emphasized once again, with it the shrines at Ise, and with them the imperial cult, whose patron deity the Sun Goddess served as reminder of the superiority of Japanese spirit and polity over all possible competitors. In literary and philosophical writing the *kokugakusha* occasionally sounded Taoist, for that tradition had always contained the Chinese antithesis to Confucian order and decorum. In philological scholarship scholars could intersect with the textual rigor of learned Confucians like Ogyū Sorai. But when they spoke of values of native deities and of national spirit they were the first ideologues of Japanism.

What matters in this context is that the national scholars, and especially Motoori, legitimized a rejection of China and Confucianism through their affirmation of Japan. In 1771, the same year that Sugita witnessed the dissection of the criminal in Edo, Motoori wrote *Naobi no mitama*, in which he proceeded to demolish and dismiss much of the Chinese tradition. He argued that the Chinese sages were nothing more than a construct of Confucian scholars designed to confuse and to impress others; they represented an effort to universalize the writings and teaching of China as though they were true at all times in all places. Nothing could be further from the truth. China was a country of disorder and violence, and the sages were simply the most successful practitioners of a special brand of deceit. The Chinese spirit, the *karagokoro*, was one of disputation and violence, and scarcely one of wisdom and of virtue. Therefore it was ridiculous to have Japanese scholars take all this so seriously. A few years later, in *Tamakatsuma*, Motoori lampooned his country's Sinophiles.

"If you ask a Confucian scholar about Japan he is not ashamed to say 'I do not know.' But if you ask him about China he would be quite ashamed to admit he did not know. This is probably because they try to make everything look Chinese, including themselves, and treat Japan like a foreign country. . . . This is one thing when talking to Japanese, but imagine telling a Chinese 'I know a lot about your country, but I don't know anything about Japan.' The Chinese would laugh, clap his hands and say, 'How can a Confucianist who doesn't know his own country expect to understand things about another country?' "

Motoori did go on to say, condescendingly, that if one had time, after studying his own Japanese tradition, it was permissible, and even desirable, to read Chinese books. How else could anyone come to realize the futility and error of the Chinese way? But one should know one's own country first.

Motoori was a formidable polemicist as well as a great scholar. In his polemics he distorted the Chinese tradition until it became a caricature of the Confucian persuasion. For the most part his target was the Japanese Confucian pedant. There were many of them, and their willingness to put China first in all matters infuriated the national scholars. To some degree also, as Professor Harootunian has argued, the national scholars used "China" more as metaphor for a set of normative values than as country, and they were really talking about ideas rather than about their source. Nevertheless it is significant that they chose their metaphor in this manner, and also that the Confucian scholars gave battle once they were aroused to the danger. The issues raised in this manner soon produced a vigorous literary polemic. It would be interesting to follow this further, as that struggle played its part in the politicization of Shintō and in the emergence of imperial loyalism. It will suffice instead to remind ourselves that the Chinese primacy was at all times forced to coexist with a lively Japanese awareness of self, and that after the late eighteenth century it lost ground rapidly. By the time of Sugita, to whom we turn next, some were prepared to contest the whole of the Chinese tradition.

4. *The Emergence of the Western Model*

The national scholars rejected the Chinese tradition of Confucian formalism, but they had little to substitute for it except an unstructured naturalism and an intuitive appreciation. Nor was their emphasis on national uniqueness and essence likely to stir them to seek other and more useful models. But by the time Motoori was writing his major works, an alternate approach to wisdom was far advanced. This was the study of the West, carried out with great difficulty with books brought by Dutch traders to Nagasaki.

It would take too long to detail this development adequately. Its main lines have been described in a number of places, and yet most of these sources only begin to suggest the richness of interest that the story has. It is surely one of the most extraordinary chapters in cultural intercourse in world history. Despite all the restrictions on movement, on enterprise, and on imports, one finds small groups of Japanese scholars working in relative and mutual isolation. In the eighteenth century they were divided into two main groups. One was the guild of interpreters at Nagasaki who serviced the official trade with the Dutch East India Company. Some twenty families held hereditary rights to the privileges involved and maintained their guild by coopting able candidates, often through adoption. There was also a much smaller group of doctors, attached to feudal lords, in residence at Edo, modern Tokyo. At the capital, Dutch learning first began to draw official interest when Arai Hakuseki interrogated an Italian Jesuit, Sidotti, who had entered the country illegally in 1709. In the 1720's, the shogun Yoshimune authorized several retainers to begin the study of Dutch for improvement of the calendar, and simultaneously relaxed the censorship of Chinese books dealing with Western learning. A half century later— in 1770—one doctor-scholar, Maeno Ryōtaku, was allowed to go "abroad" to Nagasaki to study directly with the interpreters.

The interpreters had the best opportunity to learn Dutch, but their time was also dominated by re-

1. Travellers at Hakone check station on the Tōkaidō, after Hokusai.

quirements of official duty. And even they had no
language tools or dictionaries; a laborious translation
of a dictionary was completed only in 1796. Later ver-
sions of the same work, finished in 1833, were not
permitted to be published until 1855, after the coming
of Perry.

The two groups of scholars knew about each other,
and they had occasional opportunity to meet when
senior Nagasaki interpreters accompanied the Dutch
chief merchant on his official visit to the capital. This
visit took place a total of 116 times during the two and
one half centuries of Tokugawa rule; annually after

1633, biennially after 1764, and every four years after 1790 until 1850, the last trip. The round trip from Nagasaki to Edo, carried out with all the decorum of a feudal lord's procession, usually took about 90 days; in 1787 it took 142 days. The Dutch factor, accompanied by a doctor and perhaps a secretary and his fifty or more Japanese escorts, would be lodged in the Nagasaki Inn near Nihonbashi in Edo. Here four rooms on the second floor were reserved for him; the interpreters who had accompanied him were housed on the same floor.

Edo doctors were permitted to call at the inn, usually several in a group, to pose questions to the travellers. It was an imperfect form of communication, as Ōtsuki Gentaku observed in 1794 when he noted that, unable to get the floor with a question, he would have to save it four years for the next opportunity. Some of the visitors were always eager to learn about Japan from their hosts. Kaempfer, Thunberg, and Siebold—not one of them a Dutch national—provided the West with its best accounts of Japan, and Thunberg (in 1775) and later Siebold (in the 1820's) attracted enough students to suggest the nucleus of a future scientific community.

Forms of internal communication within Japan were not always much better. Shizuki Tadao, a Nagasaki interpreter, wrote this same Ōtsuki jubilantly that a servant of his had fortunately just been conscripted as coolie for a local daimyo who was about to leave for Edo. Shizuki was seizing the chance to write Ōtsuki. "Could you send me any book you have there that describes stimulating and interesting theories of physics and astronomy, whether in Chinese or a Western language? I would particularly like to see a mathematical book on logarithms you said you were writing. I myself have a book that discusses the principle of motion in the heavens and on the earth, the reason of the rapid or slow motion, and the retrograde and stationary principles. It is called *Wetten der mid-delpuntzoekende kragten*. I have translated it."

The age of translation of which this provides evidence had in fact begun earlier, and its first real monument came as a result of the historic dissection in Edo with which I opened this lecture. The observers were two doctors, both students of Dutch, Sugita Gempaku and Maeno Ryōtaku, the man who had been permitted a stay of several months at Nagasaki in 1770. The account of that occasion is available from Sugita's memoirs:

". . . The corpse of the criminal was that of an old woman of about fifty years, nicknamed Aocha Baba, born in Kyoto. It was an old butcher who made the dissection. We had been promised an *eta* named Toramatsu, known for his skill in dissection, but because he was sick his grandfather came instead. He was ninety years old, but healthy, and he told us that he had been doing this since his youth. According to him up until this time people had left it up to him, and he had just shown them where the lungs, kidneys, and other organs were. They would pretend that they had studied the internal structure of the body directly. But the parts naturally weren't labelled, and they had to be satisfied with the way he pointed them out. He knew where everything

was, but he had not learned their proper names.
. . . Some of them turned out to be arteries, veins,
and suprarenal bodies according to our anatomical
tables. . . . We found that the structure of the lungs
and liver and the position and shape of the stomach
were quite different from what had been believed
according to old Chinese theory. . . .

"On our way home we talked with excitement
about the experiment. Since we had served our
masters as doctors, we were quite ashamed of our
ignorance of the true morphology of the human
body, which was fundamental to the medical art. In
justification of our membership in the medical profession, we made a vow to seek facts through experiment. . . . Then I suggested that we decipher the
Tafel Anatomia without the aid of interpreters in
Nagasaki, and translate it into Japanese. The next
day we met at Ryōtaku's home and began the conquest of *Tafel Anatomia*. . . .

"We translated by conjecture, word by word, and
gradually these increased in number. . . . When we
met difficult words, we thought we would get them
someday, so we marked them with a cross in a circle. How often we had to do that! Gradually we got
so we could decipher ten lines or more a day. . . .
After two or three years of hard study everything became clear to us; the joy of it was as the chewing of
sweet sugar cane."

Almost spontaneously, Sugita wrote, "a new term
rangaku (Dutch studies) arose in our society and it has
spread and become popular all over Japan."
Thus began the age of translation. By the time of

his memoirs, written in 1815 when he was in his eighties, Sugita observed that "Today so-called *rangaku* is very widespread. Some people study it earnestly, and the uneducated talk about it thoughtlessly and with exaggeration. When I think back, it is almost fifty years since some of us old men set out to foster this learning." It is different from Chinese studies, he reflects; that study had the full backing of a court that sent ambassadors to China. Why then did Dutch studies become so important? Toward the end Sugita returns to the same problem. "I never imagined that Dutch studies would become so important or make such progress. I think Chinese studies made only slow progress; but Dutch studies were more lucid and made rapid progress because they were written in plain and direct language." And still, he admits, the training in Chinese studies probably "developed our mind beforehand" also.

As one reads Sugita—his memoirs, his diary, and his dialogues—it is clear that, as Keene says of Honda, one is entering a new era. The dominance of China is at an end. Chinese wisdom is occasionally wrong, as in the morphology of the body; or impractical, and it is usually associated with conservatism and obscurantism. In a dialogue of 1775 Sugita has an interlocutor protest,

"Look here: Korea and Ryūkyū are not China, but they received the teachings of the same sages. This medical learning you are teaching, though, comes from countries on the northwest frontier of the world 9000 *ri* from China. Their language is differ-

2. Doctor Sugita Gempaku (1733-1817), pioneer student
of Western learning.

ent from China's and they don't know anything about the sages. They are the most distant of even all the barbarian countries; what possible good can their learning do us?"

In answer Sugita says it is all very well for the Chinese to profess scorn for barbarians, but look who is ruling them now! But in any case people are alike the world around, and China itself is only one small country in the Eastern Seas. True medical knowledge has to be based upon more universal grounds than upon the wisdom of a few. Furthermore, on examination it turns out that the sages' books about anatomy are not correct. On that evidence, it is far from correct to assume that one can despise the Dutch or their learning.

What did Sugita learn from his translation work? Professor Haga suggests five important lessons. The Chinese are wrong. One cannot receive traditional learning blindly or on faith, however authoritative it seems. Medicine has to be based on the facts of the body and on biology. In this regard all men are equal. And, since they are, the physician must learn to treat them all alike. None of this was directly political, yet in the long run it all had political significance. Dutch scholars could predict that government policies to maintain Japan's isolation from the Western world were doomed to failure in the face of superior Western knowledge and technology. In addition, Sugita's philosophical or social conclusions about equality—conclusions he held in common with several other leading scholars of *rangaku*—were in direct conflict with official Tokugawa policy. Sugita noted in his diary instances of striking injustice and brutality in the treatment of suspected sectarians, and in his medical practice he acted on the conclusions that he had worked out about equal worth. The consequences of this for politics were shown a little more than two decades after Sugita's death in 1817, when political conservatives were able to secure official prosecution of a group of Dutch scholars as potential subversives.

These remarks lead us well beyond Sugita, for they go straight to the mighty changes that transformed Japan after the coming of Perry. It took that long, to be sure, yet even before Sugita's death important coverage of Western technology and science was available in Japanese; by the opening decades of the nineteenth century, enquiring Japanese were coming to grips with the ideas of Galileo and of Isaac Newton. The shogunate itself began to collect Dutch books in the 1790's, and in 1811 a translation bureau was set up within the Bureau of Astronomy. Private schools patronized by eager young students like Fukuzawa Yukichi began to appear in the great cities of the country, and many of the major feudal domains did what they could to gain the advantages and to promote the study of the new learning.

The translation movement that Sugita and his friends inaugurated, and the education and experimentation to which it led, were both symbol and agent of the demolition of a world outlook that was already in process of change. It produced and fostered attitudes of mind that make the final period of Tokugawa Japan one of endless interest and vitality. The

Dutch scholars took the first steps toward the formation of what later became an open scientific community.

One must not claim too much. Concrete results of the new learning were limited and much of it was inundated under the full flood of Western science that entered the country openly, much of it in English, after the ports were opened. Confucian values and literacy in Chinese remained the bedrock of education. Yet when, in the 1850's, the Tokugawa government, having been forced to open its ports to foreign ships, prepared for the future, it brought together a group of Dutch scholars from all parts of the country to staff its new institute of barbarian learning, a center that, by several permutations, stands as the ancestor of Tokyo University. Clearly the movement that Sugita heralded was a vital development in Japanese intellectual history.

At the end of his life Sugita could look back on a career rich in rewards and in achievement. Private practice and official recognition had given him an income comparable to that of an upper samurai. He delighted in his grandchildren, his students, and his success. He ended his memoirs with a metaphor that sounded better in his day than it does in ours. "One drop of oil," he wrote, "cast into a wide pond will spread out to cover the entire surface. It was just like that; in the beginning there were only three of us— Maeno, Nakagawa, and myself—who came together to make plans for our studies. Now, when close to fifty years have elapsed, those studies have reached every corner of the country, and each year new translations seem to be brought out." "This," he goes on, "is a case of one dog barking at something, only to be echoed by ten thousand dogs barking at nothing." And finally, "What particularly delights me is the idea that, when once the way of Dutch studies is opened wide, doctors a hundred or even a thousand years from now will be able to master real medicine and use it to save people's lives. When I think of the public benefits this will bring, I cannot help dancing and springing for joy."

II

Wisdom
Sought Throughout the
World

Sugita Gempaku had an optimistic view of his world and society in his last years, but the half century that followed his death in 1817 was full of alarm and frustration for his successors. The alarm was the product of their increasing awareness of the approach of the West and of their country's unpreparedness to deal with that approach. The frustration was the product of their government's efforts to contain the knowledge and discussion of that approach and the danger it contained within authorized channels. The Tokugawa authorities tried to extend central control at the expense of their vassals, and they tried to control private inquiry and discussion. They were no more successful in these attempts than they were in efforts to deal with economic distress and with the popular unrest that resulted.

The result was to politicize a generation. Each of the intellectual traditions of eighteenth-century Japan made its contribution to the volatile politics of the

1850's and 1860's: Confucianism through its emphasis
on duty and loyalty, national learning with its venera-
tion of emperor and sacred country, and Dutch studies with their documentation of the national danger.
Fifteen years after the coming of Perry, the shogun
had laid down his office and a new leadership had issued a five-point pledge of reform in the name of a boy
emperor.

The title for this discussion of the 1870's is drawn
from the famous Five Article pledge which the young
emperor issued in April 1868. The evil customs of the
past would be ended, he said, and "Knowledge shall
be sought throughout the world in order to strengthen
the foundations of imperial rule." The symbol of that
search is a great government learning mission that was
sent around the world in 1871-1873, one whose report
was completed in 1875 by Kume Kunitake. For
Kume, as for Sugita Gempaku, we also have memoirs
recorded in old age when he was ninety, memoirs that
were published in two volumes in 1934.

Kume Kunitake was born in 1839, and he died in
1931. Those dates span the period from the Opium
War in China to the Manchurian Incident, and they
may be taken to symbolize a shift in the image held of
China, from cultural ideal to military prize. For Japan
those same dates bridge a period in which the Tokugawa structure gave way under domestic discontent
and foreign threat, to be rebuilt on Western lines to
preserve national independence and to secure international equality. At the time of Kume's death, Japan
was asserting hegemony in East Asia in a futile effort
to contain change at home and to control it on the

continent. For Kume himself these years began with
education in traditional Confucianism and continued
with firsthand experience of the West: they also
brought personal experience of the incompatibility of
scientific rationality with aspects of Japan's new imperial ideology.

1. The Late Tokugawa Years

The two decades between the coming of Perry
and the Iwakura mission were full of political fireworks, and, in the excitement of the extremism gener-
ated by the foreign pressure, it is easy to lose sight of
deeper currents. In writing about the career of
Sakamoto Ryōma I did my share in focusing attention
on the political events of that period. In longer perspective, however, there were other and deeper currents as the Japanese changed their views of the world.
It may be that the principal contribution of the political violence was to bring increasing numbers of Japanese to focus their attention on the problem of how
their society should be restructured.

The news of the Opium War did its part to discredit
the idea of Chinese superiority. Its revelation of
Chinese military weakness struck particularly at Japanese conservatives, to whom the Chinese example was
most important. We have much evidence of their dis-
comfiture and distress. Chinese publications that discussed the problem found quick response and a wide
audience in Japan, where every educated person could
read them. Indeed, one of the remarkable things

about the period is that writers like Wei Yüan may have had more impact on their Japanese readers than on their Chinese. (The same may have been the case in earlier years with Chinese-language discussions of Western science produced by the Jesuit mission.) Dutch reports from Nagasaki reinforced what was in the Chinese accounts, and the word of China's defeat soon produced a sense of impending crisis in Japan. It is true that, a few centuries earlier, educated Japanese had also been aware of the Manchu victory over the Ming, but the Opium War was different; the new threat was non-traditional: it came by sea, it could be expected to continue on to Japan, and there were many more educated Japanese to be concerned than there had ever been before.

The sudden relevance of study of the West served to spur interest in it. It will be remembered that its legitimization within the national tradition had already begun. A half century earlier Hirata Atsutane had anticipated a new eclecticism. Chinese learning, he wrote in 1811, was only one of a half dozen or more categories. The most important of these for him was, of course, Japanese Shintō. Chinese learning was another; Buddhist learning was broader than Chinese, and Dutch learning more useful. But Japanese learning embraced all of these traditions. "Japanese," he concluded, "should study all the different kinds of learning," for, properly understood, all were Japanese.

The arrival of Perry was followed by steps to institutionalize Western learning, which now became a path to official employment and a direct concern of government. The Institute for the Study of Barbarian

Books, soon renamed the Institute for Western Books
and then the Institute for Development (*Kaiseijo*), illustrated the way in which the shogunate and its major
vassals set to work to utilize the knowledge of the
West. The Tokugawa institute became a national effort, and it hired men from all parts of the country.
Elsewhere leading barons also competed for the services of outstanding "barbarian experts." On every
hand there was a sudden intensification in the subsidi-
zation of Western studies.

The new diplomatic relations and problems next
produced a need for foreign travel. Beginning with the
first embassy to the United States in 1860 to ratify the
Harris Commercial Treaty, the 1860's saw a quicken-
ing pace in the frequency, size, and seriousness of
missions to the Western world. The accounts of the
Japanese travellers give a fascinating perspective on
their growing sophistication.

The original embassy to Washington included a
total of seventy-seven men. Walt Whitman saluted
their New York appearance in *A Broadway Pageant*,
and the vice ambassador, Muragaki, Awaji no kami,
recorded his impressions in his diary, *Kōkai Nikki*.
The vice ambassador's notations show that he is still a
simple tourist. There is no real effort to see much of
economic or technological importance, and his contacts are largely limited to the official round of state
entertainments. He shows a faint distaste for bizarre
features of American society like the presence of
women at state occasions. A visit to the Senate produces astonishment at the proceedings of the Congress. "One of the members was on his feet," he notes,

3. Ambassadors who led the first mission to the United States in 1860. Vice Ambassador Muragaki on left.

"haranguing at the top of his voice, and gesticulating wildly like a madman. When he sat down, his example was followed by another, and yet another. Upon our inquiring what it was all about, we were informed that all the affairs of State were thus publicly discussed by the members, and that the Vice-President made his decision, after he heard the opinion of every member." A trip to the Smithsonian brings horror at the sight of mummies shown alongside birds and animals. "These foreigners," the ambassador notes, "are not nicknamed barbarians for nothing." Most intriguing of all, perhaps, is a very superficial but revealing comment made when the ship stopped in Angola on the way home: the natives have some resemblance to Buddhist images, and "we come to discover that the natives of India and Africa both belong to one and the same tribe, of whom that Buddha must have been a chieftain." How absurd, the diarist goes on, that the Japanese have for so long worshipped such primitive people. The new structure of relative national prestige is not yet built, but the old hierarchy of respect is clearly in process of dissolution.

Two years later another embassy left Japan for a much more ambitious tour. Its purpose was to seek delay in the opening of additional treaty ports in Japan, and in this it failed. But in the secondary purpose of educating its members about the West it was successful. Its members included thirty-eight men ranging from seventeen (the youngest interpreter) to fifty-six in age, and among them were several scholars who had taken part in the earlier mission. Fukuzawa Yukichi, Mitsukuri Shūhei, and Fukuchi Genichirō,

"Dutch scholars" and Western experts, were publicists of great importance for the enlightenment movement of the future. The embassy members worked much harder than the earlier group, and they saw much more. Their detailed reports on individual countries were augmented by individual accounts compiled by some members on their return. Of these Fukuzawa's famous *Seiyō jijō* (Conditions in the West), which sold hundreds of thousands of copies, played a major role in educating Japanese in the years that lay ahead. To one anti-foreign zealot, for instance, Fukuzawa's account of the American revolution served as encouraging evidence that Japan's problems were not unique, and that modern organization and participation could provide a solution. As Nakaoka Shintarō put it, "The oppression of the English king became more heavy every day, and the American people suffered. At that point, a man named Washington complained of the people's hardships. . . . He closed the country and drove out the barbarians. . . . The thirteen colonies gained their independence and then became a strong country. . . ."

In the reports compiled by the travellers in 1862, the ambivalences of Western society receive mention for the first time. The state of the industrial city with its urban poor emerges, and the gradations of national power and influence begin to come into focus. France is beautiful, especially the new Paris of Napolean III; but England, for all its dirt and noise, has more power. Paris may be a Kyoto, but London is the Edo (modern Tokyo); "When it comes to trains, telegraphs, hospitals, schools, armories and industries,

England must have twenty times what France does."
A reflective poem compares this to a Mongolia grown
more powerful than the cultured Central Kingdom.

The members of this and the next few missions returned to a Japan that was still not sure of the path it
should follow in its reconstruction. Often they were
not welcome at home, and occasionally their lives
were in danger. For the most part the top men disappeared into obscurity. But the lower-ranking men, the
interpreters and the experts, became leaders in the enlightenment movement of the 1870's. Mission followed mission, and a sixth was abroad at the time of
the shogun's fall in 1867. By then a number of feudal
lords had smuggled students overseas to study. The
Tokugawa government itself had commissioned returned students to draw up a kind of constitution for
the last shogun at the time of his resignation.

All this activity was fully as important as the political fireworks of those same years. It also helped to
create a favorable view of Japan in foreign countries.
The Chinese statesman Li Hung-chang, for instance,
wrote to propose for his own country forthright measures of change like those he thought he saw in Japan,
and Japanese travellers reported with satisfaction that
Japan was considered more progressive than China.

The travel of the 1860's had a number of important
results. One was a growing concern with Japan as a
country. In the new international world there could
be only limited tolerance for the divisions of the late
feudal Japan. One finds no Tokugawa consciousness
in these diaries and writings; it is Japan that counts and
the country's future is at stake. "In olden days," the

vice-ambassador's account of 1860 begins, "envoys
were sent to China, but that is only a neighboring
country. . . . I realized that failure in accomplishing
this unprecedented task . . . would constitute an ir-
reparable disgrace to our country." His first poem ex-
presses the hope that

> "From now on, the bright moonlight of our
> country
> Will be admired by the peoples of the strange
> lands."

After the reception by President Buchanan, he
proudly calls upon the barbarians to turn their faces
upward to contemplate "This glory of our Eastern
Empire of Japan." Walt Whitman, of course, got it a
little differently:

> "Superb-faced Manhattan
> Comrade Americans!—to us, then at last,
> the Orient comes."

Equally certain was the rapid move down in the
hierarchy of prestige for China. This was in part the
product of a knowledge of China's repute abroad, and
it was speeded by Japanese visits to the treaty-port
fringe of China. What they saw in Shanghai convinced the travellers that no comparable loss of
sovereignty could be allowed to take place in Japan.

There was also a growing sophistication about the
West. It was less an undifferentiated mass, and gradually becoming an area that permitted and in fact required selection. But it was not yet structured; that
would require more travel, more observation, and

more experience. This came with the early Meiji missions.

2. *Travellers of the 1870's*

The setting within which the learning missions of the 1870's took place was made radically different by the pledge of 1868 to seek learning throughout the world. It should, however, be remembered that the 1868 pledge was for long-range purposes, and that it was meant to reassure the treaty powers and the Japanese elite. Japanese commoners received rather different advice from the local sign boards from which they got their instructions. These were redone to accommodate traditional outlooks to the new circumstances of the times. They contained cryptic reminders of Confucian morality, forbad rebellion and desertion, maintained the proscription of Christianity, and ruled out attacks on foreigners. Here there was less renunciation of the evil customs of the past.

As knowledge of the West increased with direct contact, it became possible to rank Western countries and institutions for the purpose of emulation. A hierarchy of prestige was probable because of the structured society of late Tokugawa feudalism, and the Japanese tendency to make such judgments was strengthened by the teaching about stages of progress and development that were found in Western books.

The most influential transmitter of this Western teaching of progress was Fukuzawa Yukichi, who was now a veteran of three trips to the Western world. The booklets of his famous *Gakumon no susume* (The Encouragement of Learning), written between 1872 and 1880, may have reached sales of close to a million copies, and could therefore have been read by a very high percentage of adult Japanese who were literate. Fukuzawa was both prolific and popular, so much so that for a time all books about the West were called "Fukuzawa books" (*Fukuzawabon*). *Gakumon no susume*, which helped to confirm his fame, was a call to initiative and effort. Its famous opening sentence, "Heaven does not create one man above or below another man," constituted a ringing endorsement of the Meiji government's moves to abolish class distinctions, phrased in terms of the eighteenth-century thought Fukuzawa had already transmitted through his translation of the Declaration of Independence in his earlier *Seiyō jijō*. The 1872 Fukuzawa quickly went on to recognize substantial differences between individuals, though he credited these to effort and diligence. It was so also with countries. "There are strong and wealthy nations which are called mature civilizations," Fukuzawa said, and "there are also poor and weak nations which are primitive or underdeveloped. In general, the nations of Europe and America illustrate the first category, those of Asia and Africa the second." A few years later, in a history of civilization, Fukuzawa presented a scheme of three stages of development: countries were savage (*yaban*), semideveloped (*hankai*, which included China and Japan), and civilized (*bunmei*). The last-named had curiosity and science in addition to culture and literature. It was clear to Fukuzawa's readers how Japan could climb that final step.

The Iwakura mission of 1871-1873 provided government leaders with a twenty-one-month world tour during which they had the opportunity to see for themselves. This was no ordinary junket. Prince Iwakura Tomomi, who headed the group as Ambassador Plenipotentiary, was the most prestigious member of the new government. Vice ambassadors included the powerful Ōkubo Toshimichi and Kido Takayoshi, leaders of the coalition that had brought down the Tokugawa government, as well as Itō Hirobumi, who was to be a principal architect of the modern state structure. It is little wonder that some doubted the wisdom of sending such central figures off for so long, or that the ambassadors took the precaution of having their colleagues pledge not to institute major changes without discussion during their absence. As each government department attached members to extend its coverage, the mission grew until the total number of secretaries, commissioners, and officers neared fifty. But even this party was only the core for a larger group. Recent feudal lords of Chōshū, Saga, Fukuoka, and Kanazawa came, each accompanied by retainers, as did court nobles Madenokōji and Shimizudani. The Hokkaido Colonization Office added representatives. Five young women were included as pioneers in Western education for females, and several dozen additional students were attached for placing in Western schools. Thus the total group that set out numbered around one hundred. In a farewell ceremony the mission was charged by the emperor to visit the countries with which Japan had now resumed contact and to observe and report on aspects of their institutions. The still

4. Iwakura Tomomi (1825-1883),
court noble and leader of the
early Meiji government,
at the time he led mission
to the United States and Europe,
1871-1873.

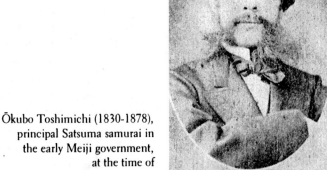

5. Ōkubo Toshimichi (1830-1878),
principal Satsuma samurai in
the early Meiji government,
at the time of
the Iwakura mission.

unfinished Yokohama Railway station was used for the sendoff, and a Meiji artist in the Western style did his best to capture the color and ceremonial of the departure from the pier.

Of the principal members only Itō had been abroad before. At lower levels several anti-foreign types were included quite deliberately, in the hope of educating them. This was only partly successful; one, Murata Shimpachi, stayed on an additional year in France for military education and returned just in time to take command under Saigō in the Satsuma Rebellion, while another, Yasuba Yasukazu, had such a terrible time with Arabic numerals, confusing even the floors, to say nothing of hotel room numbers, that he finally persuaded the chief ambassador to relent and let him go home. Foreign travel did not work with everyone.

In the vast majority of cases, however, travel produced a convergence of views in favor of steady but moderate reform. Radicals found themselves sobered by realization of the distance between Japan and the Western world, and conservatives realized that opposition to change was hopeless. These conclusions tallied with the advice of foreign advisers whom the Japanese respected. The English minister, Harry Parkes, warned of precipitous measures; the German doctor Erwin Baelz kept reminding his hosts how far they had to go; and General Grant, who visited Japan on his world tour, warned that liberties once given could never again be retracted. A few years later Herbert Spencer, when sounded out on the wisdom of intermarriage, returned a considered opinion, based on his knowledge of cattle breeding, against mixing different strains. "My advice," he wrote in 1892, "is strongly conservative in all directions, and I end by saying as I began—keep other races at arm's length as much as possible."

The official record of the Iwakura mission was provided by Kume Kunitake, a Confucian scholar-samurai from Saga. From his official five-volume account and from the reminiscences that he dictated at the age of ninety it is possible to piece together some very clear-headed impressions.

In common with most of his generation, Kume restructured his hierarchy of countries, and the West came out on top. Its countries and peoples seemed less sluggish and passive than those of the East, and their attainments were higher. The criteria for this judgment, as Marlene Mayo points out, were in good part materialistic. The goods produced by a society were a good index of its state of civilization. There was also the criterion of distribution; one might establish a correlation between the people's share of the overall wealth and the state of civilization. Furthermore, countries could also be rated by the way their institutions mobilized the energies of their people.

The embassy's stay of two hundred and five days in the United States provided its first, and in fact its longest, period of observation of the non-Japanese world. The American visit was long partly because of the distances to be covered and especially because of a delay caused by the return of two vice ambassadors to Japan to secure more explicit credentials for diplomatic negotiations—credentials of which no real use was made, since negotiation took second place to ob-

6. Departure of Iwakura mission from Yokohama in 1871.
Iwakura (in court robes), Ōkubo and Kido, on the fantail of
the launch taking them to their ship.

servation. But the long stay in the United States also seemed appropriate because of the importance that the American example posed for early Meiji Japan.

Kume's account makes much of the happy combination of natural resources and human will that built the United States. The latter he credited to initiative and independence, the character of a society assembled from people from all parts of Europe. The United States, he wrote, was in fact the development ground for the independent-minded of Europe. Its people had voluntarily and wisely abandoned the diffuse political units of their earlier statehood and had entered into a centralized state, in good measure because of the need to act effectively in foreign affairs. As with the newer unity of Germany, the American commitment to a central government provided a commonality which underlay the obvious differences of these two modernizing states, and provided clear lessons for a Japan that was in process of abandoning its own feudal divisions.

America's experience was also testimony to the strength of associative, republican institutions, and its people were remarkable for their strong faith and high vitality. Yet the ambassadors never forgot the importance of building for themselves, and they were determined to distinguish the core of a modernized polity from the form in which it might be contained. The American electoral system raised doubts for them about the ability of people to choose, and of leaders to advocate, the wise above the merely popular and cheap. In the final analysis it was the combination of will, resources, and productivity that commended the

United States to Iwakura and his party. These same considerations made America a magnet for Japanese students in the early Meiji decades.

Great Britain stood to offer even more examples in its combination of size, age, and productivity, and to it the embassy devoted one hundred and twenty-two days, and Kume 443 of his pages, as compared with 397 for the United States. Germany and France each received half this space of exposition, and Russia, for all its size, one quarter. Indeed, in civilization Russia seemed at the lowest level among Western countries. Its goods were crude, its trade and industry were dominated by foreigners, its wealth was monopolized by an autocratic government and aristocracy, and its peasants lived lives of shocking poverty. Civilization seemed almost to decline as one moved east in Europe.

Kume and his associates did their best to look beneath the surface of the countries they visited and they concerned themselves with deeper currents. It seemed to them that the underlying difference between the East and West was the restless, Faustian spirit of Western peoples and their intensely competitive attitude about material things. Their nature was to desire intensely, while the East Asians were less insistent. "In Europe they say 'justice' and 'society' are the essence of government," Kume wrote, "but our Eastern notions are ultimately derived from virtue and morality, while theirs are based on the need to protect property." In a sense this distinction stemmed from the Western conviction of human nature as evil, with the consequent need to regulate competition, and from the Eastern conviction of human nature as fundamentally good.

Whatever the roots of these differences, however, it was clear that international society, now dominated by the West, was something of a jungle in which "countries are friendly in the sun but hostile in the shade." It is true that this thought had occurred to some of the ambassadors a good deal earlier. Kido had written in 1868 that "the law of nations is merely a tool for the conquest of the weak," and a year later Iwakura wrote his colleagues that "in the final analysis these countries are our enemies. Every foreign country tries to become another country's superior." Similarly, Fukuzawa Yukichi would write in 1878 that "a handful of Treaties of Friendship are not worth a basket of ammunition." Clearly, Japan had to adjust to this and build up its strength.

Yet the ambassadors returned with the conclusion that the immediate danger to Japan's independence was less pressing than some had thought. Russia, for instance, was much too backward and too absorbed in internal problems to be a threat. Rather than prepare for an early conflict, Japan should set its house in order and work its way up in the international hierarchy of respect and prestige. The "West" to which it must conform was now more clearly differentiated, and in its variety there was choice for a modernizing Japan. In terms of current history, the recent unifications of Germany and Italy seemed to offer analogous examples, and in fact German and Austrian precedents were soon to be the objects of close study. But the adoption of particular institutions was by no means immediate or automatic, and as the embassy divided into teams for detailed investigation of education, government, and economic development each group found items of particular interest in different countries.

One thing that struck the travellers in each of the developed countries they visited was the respect and importance that was attached to its past. The progress of the present was rooted deep in the historical experience of Western people; indeed, Kume wrote, "its origin lies in the spirit of love for tradition." The public museums of the West had no parallel in the East, and they were instruments for the enlightenment of the popular mind. "By progress we do not mean tossing out the old and striving for the new," Professor Mayo quotes Kume; "a country develops by the accumulation of customs; it polishes the beauty of the past."

Another was the realization of changes that would have to be made in Japan. Japan would have to end its ban on Christianity, for this drew reproachful comments wherever the travellers went. The Japanese developed respect for the civic virtues of Christianity, at least as they saw it in the United States and in Protestant Europe. Although Kume expressed astonishment at the acceptance of supernaturalism in Biblical Christianity, he was impressed by the role, if not by the content, of that faith in American life. The formal deference to Christian teachings, the presence of a house of worship in every hamlet, church attendance on Sunday, and general knowledge of the Bible, all seemed to him in decided contrast to the fact that Confucianism and Buddhism were spent forces in East Asia. On the other hand, as the mission moved on into Catholic and Orthodox countries, the travellers were astonished by the power and wealth of institutionalized Christianity. The state church of Russia in particular dismayed Kume. Professor Mayo quotes his contrast between Japan's Buddhist temples and the cathedrals of Europe: "The Honganji is to the great temples of Europe as a thatched hut to a mansion. I was astonished at the extent to which Western religions squander the people's wealth in churches." And as for Russia, "The more backward a country, the more powerful is the influence of religious superstition and the more likely the people are to worship idols and animals." Further, he decided that while the upper classes everywhere made a show of honoring religion, in actuality they used it to strengthen obedience to authority. It is clear that the mission's conclusion that restrictions on Christianity would have to go did not result from a weakening of Confucian rationalism. Christianity puzzled and impressed most of the travellers. Sasaki Takuyuki thought it clear that social customs could not be reformed without adherence to religion, but Kido Takayoshi wondered why it was that Europeans and Americans were so enthusiastic about religion.

Another conviction gained was that something would have to be done about representative institutions in Japan to build a better consensus for government actions. Such institutions seemed closely correlated with the state of advancement in European countries. Kido's statement about this problem on his return is a famous one. He argued from the experience of Poland that lack of popular participation could be fatal to national independence. Japan was not yet ready for parliamentary government, but it should consider the emperor's Charter Oath of 1868 as the foundation of a future constitution. The interesting thing about this is that it was the trip that had made Kido fully aware of this role for the Charter Oath, even though he had participated in its formulation himself. Kume relates that during a lull in Washington he set to work translating the American Constitution (with great problems for terms like *habeas corpus*, justice, and the like). Kido looked in on him often, and as the work progressed their talk included speculation about the future. One day Kume observed that political changes of the order that Japan was experiencing ought to be formalized in a state charter, especially in view of the emperor's solemn pledge. Kido picked up his ears; "What did the emperor pledge?" "The five article Charter Oath," Kume replied. Kido clapped his hands: "Of course! That was in there! Have you got a copy here?" The next day Kido appeared again. "Last night I read that Charter Oath very carefully, time after time," he said; "it really is a superb document. We can never allow that spirit to change. I will certainly support it for the rest of my life." Foreign travel thus gave new significance to earlier phrases and helped to guide future decisions.

While first-rank leaders returned to their Tokyo responsibilities, younger colleagues could be spared for longer periods of study in the West. Future prime ministers like General Katsura and Prince Saionji,

7. Kido Takayoshi, principal Chōsnū
leader in the early Meiji government,
at the time of the Iwakura mission.

both of whom moved to the front in the early years of
the twentieth century, experienced long periods of
seasoning in Europe in the 1870's. They were only the
most eminent of a small army of Japanese students
who went overseas to study in the years after the Meiji
Restoration. Between 1868 and 1902 11,248 passports
were issued for study overseas, a figure that indicates
the first great student migration of modern times. (The
second would be that of Chinese students to Japan in
the first decades of the twentieth century.) The United

States led in attracting over half of these students for reasons of proximity, cost, and challenge. The encouragement and support of American missionaries and teachers undoubtedly contributed to this total also. But within a decade after the return of the Iwakura mission the same government figures reveal that virtually all officially sponsored students were being sent to Germany, in accordance with decisions taken about the appropriateness of Central European models in science, government, law, and military organization. Although the students coming to America remained more numerous, they tended also to play more modest roles in their society upon their return to Japan. The Iwakura mission of 1871 had among its responsibilities an investigation of the way Japanese students abroad were preparing themselves for future service. For a brief moment the Education Ministry was spending as much as 21 percent of its budget on study abroad. More prudent planners soon cut this sharply. Schools within Japan were strengthened with generous use of well-paid foreign teachers, and by the 1890's those teachers had for the most part been replaced by their students. By then the Japanese educational structure was in place, and official support of study abroad changed from a crash program to train individuals in areas of knowledge in which Japan was lacking to a more general willingness to enable mature scholars to reinforce the solid foundation of Western knowledge they had acquired in Japanese institutions. By that time the members of the Iwakura mission were recognized for the work they had done. We can cite Tsuda Umeko, one of the girl students of 1871 who had returned to found Japan's first women's college, and Itō Hirobumi, designer of the Meiji Constitution, diplomat, prime minister, and chief minister of his emperor, and showered with honors as various as the highest titles in the Japanese peerage, Knight of the Bath from the England which he had first visited secretly in 1863, and an honorary doctorate from Yale.

The reverse side of the travellers' new appreciation of the West was the confirmation of their gloomy conclusions about the East. Alexandria, Suez, Hong Kong, Canton, and Shanghai were minor stops on the way home, and occasioned only superficial reflections on the unfortunate state of affairs in societies that seemed unjust, slothful, and corrupt. In *Gakumon no susume* Fukuzawa had already castigated the Chinese for their stubborn indifference to other countries. Kume's chronicle, too, showed little sense of kinship with other Asians. In the port cities he visited, he contrasted the orderly foreign sectors with the impoverished native areas, and he was particularly scornful of the prevalence of opium in China. The respect that Japanese literati had long held for Chinese civilization and elegance did not survive these first-hand impressions. Among ordinary Japanese it may have lingered longer, but there is no doubt that the personal experiences and impressions of thousands of Japanese conscripts who served in the armies in the wars against China and Russia served to diffuse and fix an image of condescension and even contempt for the sectors of the continent their presence had helped to blight.

One can probably anticipate these twentieth-century emotions in the clear progression from Kume's unfavorable impressions of the 1870's to Fukuzawa's famous warning ten years later that Japan should "part with Asia." "Although China and Korea are our neighbors," he wrote in 1885, "this fact should make no difference in our relations with them. We should deal with them as Westerners do. If we keep bad company, we cannot avoid a bad name. In my heart I favor breaking off with the bad company of East Asia." Thus the hierarchy of prestige had been decisively restructured. About the same time, Itō Hirobumi expressed similar embarrassment when the terminology for the new nobility was worked out in 1884. "I am distressed that it seems unavoidable to use the Chinese system," he wrote a subordinate; "if you have any other ideas, let me have them."

To sum up: The ambassadors and their contemporaries developed a highly differentiated view of the West. They avoided slavish submission to any single country, and they saw and recorded the shortcomings of each. As a whole, the West moved far ahead of the traditional models of East Asia. But the ultimate criterion for selection and emulation was the presumed benefit for the Meiji state. In their nationalism the Iwakura ambassadors and their contemporaries were guided by the wording of the Charter Oath, which specified that knowledge was to be sought throughout the world, "so as to strengthen the foundations of Imperial Rule."

A historian has to guard against letting his enthusiasm for his subject distort its importance. The Iwakura mission was the symbol, and not the source, of many movements of the times. During its absence the caretaker government in Tokyo moved forward vigorously on a number of reforms. The student tide to the West, and especially to America and to England, began earlier and continued after the mission. Perhaps the mission's most direct contribution was the new awareness it gave its members of the need for caution in foreign affairs. And even this would have counted for little if the ambassadors had not found their government jobs waiting for them in Tokyo despite their long absence. In some ways, this may be the most remarkable thing of all about the embassy. In how many developing countries of our own day would the top leadership risk absence from the scene of power for a period of more than a year and a half? This tells volumes about the confidence of the Japanese in the underlying stability and solidity of their society, and in their ability to set and enforce the pace of institutional change.

3. The New Japanism

After the return of the Iwakura mission to Japan, the wisdom that had been collected began to be put to work. The ambassadors' conclusions about the strength of the West were translated into a decision against military adventures in Korea, and this brought on a split in the leadership—partly between those who had been abroad and those who had not—and that split in turn was followed by samurai revolts. Advocates of immediate constitutional government, most of whom had also not been abroad, provided a radical

opposition to gradualism, and that complicated the
orderly process toward reform from above preferred by
the government leaders. The government usually had
its own way, but its efforts to secure the foreign approval that was essential for revision of the unequal
treaties that had been forced upon Japan led it to spon-
sor forms of Westernization that provided targets for its
domestic critics. For some of these it seemed that the
careful selectivity advocated by the Iwakura report was
being abandoned.

The Europeanization movement of the 1880's represented the high-water mark of admiration for the institutions and manners of the West. Japanese students
went abroad in large numbers, and in their diaries and
reminiscences one senses the insecurity and awkward-
ness of their realization of Japan's low standing in the
international hierarchy of advanced countries. Often
the Japanese diplomats and long-term residents they
encountered abroad helped to shock them into this
awareness. Mori Ōgai's *German Diary* opens with a
revealing comment made by Minister Aoki Shūzō
when the young student paid a courtesy call on him.
"What are you studying?" "Hygiene." "You won't
find much use for it when you go home. People who
still have thongs for clogs between their toes have no
use for hygiene." Foreign Minister Inoue Kaoru put it
baldly in 1887: "Let us change our empire into a
European-style empire. Let us change our people into
a European-style people. Let us create a new European-style empire on the Eastern sea." Mutsu
Munemitsu, returning from Europe in 1886, said it
would be necessary to change everything, from intan-

8. Late Meiji mix of Japanese and Western clothing.
Buyers inspecting picture postcards.

gibles like education and morals to the concrete things
of everyday life such as clothing, food, and houses.
These confessions of cultural inferiority went well beyond those of the ambassadors in the 1870's, and they
soon produced counter-currents of reaffirmation of
Japanese cultural identity.

The new Japanism freed itself from the Chinese
image, but it also appropriated a good deal of it
quietly. Its official formulation came with the Imperial Rescript on Education of 1890, a statement that is
reminiscent to some degree of the Sacred Edicts of
the K'ang-hsi and Yung-cheng emperors of Ch'ing

China. This powerful document, which was designed
to serve as the center of morality and focus of ritual in
the public schools, held up the Confucian virtues of
loyalty and filiality as "the glory of the fundamental
character of our Empire" and "the source of our education." Traditional virtues were linked to "public
good" and "common interests," and reinforced each
other to "guard and maintain the prosperity of our
Imperial Throne." These principles, the edict pointed
out correctly, were in no wise new, but "indeed the
teaching bequeathed by our Imperial ancestors." Thus
the search for wisdom had in good measure come full
circle.

The intellectual formulations of the new Japanism
were worked out by a group of journalist-philosophers.
Geographical and aesthetic interpretations of Japanese
values were combined in a Hegelian view of history by
a brilliant young ghost writer and disciple of Miyake
Setsurei who went on to become Japan's leading
Sinologist. Naitō Konan drew on all the traditions of
which we have made mention—Chinese philology,
Japanese loyalism, and Western science—to argue
that civilizations move from starting points to new
centers. Just as that of the Near East had reached its
apogee in Western Europe, that of East Asia had
originated in China to come to bloom in neighboring
Japan. Europe, however, was already in decline, and
Europeans were becoming aware of the hollowness of
their materialism. This situation contained an un-
usual opportunity for Japan. "Japan's mission is not to
introduce Western civilization to China, nor to preserve the Chinese curios and sell them to the West.

Japan's mission is to promote Japanese culture with the taste unique to Japan and to brighten the universe. Since Japan is located in the East and since China is the largest neighbor in the East, Japan must begin its task in China." In these sentences of Naitō's, sentences which date from the 1890's, we have the germ of an altogether new sense of world view and mission for Japan.

But what of Kume, the chronicler of the Iwakura mission? He lived a very long time, as the memoirs he dictated at ninety suggest, but his career pattern was full of irony that illustrated the switches that took place. After his return in 1873 he devoted several years to the five-volume account of the Iwakura embassy which he finally published in 1878. The Emperor expressed his favor by granting Kume 500 yen, a sum he wisely invested in Tokyo real estate. His work was immediately praised as the best travel account of its day. It was much more, of course; its sharply focused appraisals of Western countries and phenomena mirrored the impressions of his generation. In 1878 Kume joined the Bureau of Historical Compilation, and in 1888 he occupied a chair of Japanese history at the Imperial University in Tokyo. Now his Confucian rationalism and Western iconoclasm led him to take a scholarly and critical position on the authenticity of early Japanese texts. In 1891 he published a cool appraisal of Shintō as a dated ritual. With this he soon found himself in trouble with the new Japanism. The chronicler of the 1870's became one of the first victims of the new orthodoxy of the 1890's, and he was forced into early retirement from the state university.

Thereafter Kume taught at Waseda University and continued to write accounts of early Japanese history. But he repented of his earlier radicalism.

In the first lecture I was able to end with Sugita Gempaku's astonishment at the changes that his life had brought. It seemed to him that the ripple he had started with his translation of a medical work had grown into a formidable tide. In 1930 Kume was also sure that his life had witnessed great changes; indeed, he thought them unprecedented in world history. "My life has been lived in the most interesting period of history since the beginning of time," he said, "and I was lucky enough to be able to see it from the finest seat." His specific comments on contemporary world history are also of considerable interest: "When we went abroad in 1872," he said, "European civilization was at its zenith and there was nothing to match the self image of the English. But in our lifetime, in a little more than fifty or sixty years, we have seen the English begin to decline." The roots of that decline, Kume felt, were in Western materialism. He hoped for better things for his Japan, and he could imagine no more fortunate time to be alive than the life span he had known. "My first thirty years," he reminisced, "were decades that witnessed the dissolution of feudal institutions that had been transmitted from antiquity; horizons were limited to small localities, which seemed a veritable universe. My second thirty years saw Japan become united and join the ranks of the great powers, and in my last thirty years I have seen Japan work as one of those powers to maintain the peace of the world." He died, as I said, in 1931.

9. Kume Kunitake (1839-1931), chronicler of the Iwakura mission, in his last years.

III

Japan's Search for Role
in the
Twentieth Century

At the end of his life Kume expressed himself in optimistic terms about Japan's role in maintaining world peace, but within months of his death in 1931 the Japanese seizure of Manchuria had opened an era of violence that lasted until the surrender in 1945. His expectations of continued progress proved as mistaken as those of Sugita Gempaku; self-doubt, social unrest, and perceptions of international danger combined to politicize a generation of activists and to plunge the country into war. The changes that followed Kume's death were even more cataclysmic than those he had experienced during his eventful life.

By the twentieth century the synthesis of the Meiji era that had been symbolized by the close cohesion of the small leadership group had given way to a setting in which professional bureaucrats and special-interest groups dominated what seemed, on the surface, an orderly progress toward more liberal outlooks and institutions. Nevertheless the underlying emphasis was more often on conservation than on innovation. Government ministries and policies had shown their fear of social change and of possible radicalism as early as the years after the Russo-Japanese War. In the decade after World War I, as socialism and communism came closer, and as the economy plunged into depression after the boom years of the war, the government responded by attempts to define orthodoxy and to police thought.

In this process the imperial institution, which had been an agent of modernization and national unity in a Japan that was emerging from feudal divisions, became a bulwark against further change, a symbol of conformity, and the definition of nationality and orthodoxy. It was supported by a generation that had been indoctrinated in its majesty throughout its formative years. The sovereign stood aloof and distant, less personal and more sacrosanct than the Meiji Emperor, who had rallied his countrymen through exhortation and by inspection tours to every corner of the land. To be sure, the imperial institution could be used in many ways, for it was an essential part of every argument. Yoshino Sakuzō, the leading theorist of parliamentary government, capped his argument by asserting the identity of popular and imperial will. The fascist radical Kita Ikki posed the need for a "people's emperor" who, stripped of the wealth with which the government had tried to tie him to the plutocracy, would be supported by a parliament of patriots. Military radicals proposed a "Shōwa" imperial restoration that would complete the work of Meiji by throwing off the Western and capitalist trappings of the modern state. But the ruling conservatives had the best claim on the institution's sanctions and support, and successfully resisted limitation or extension of its intervention in the political process.

Yoshino's idealistic vision of parliamentary progress often seemed to be contradicted by the realities of special-interest politics. Kita Ikki's writings were laundered by scandalized censors, but they circulated in handwritten copies within the military establishment. The military, as part of the larger society, naturally drew upon its fissures to warn of social unrest and external dangers. Among young hotheads internal dangers resonated with the perception of external opportunities to radicalize and to politicize. As a result, young officers, laying claim to the legacy of young samurai who brought about the Meiji Restoration, became the locomotive force of political instability. Their more conservative superiors profited from this instability to strengthen their own position and ended by gaining direction of Japan's policies.

Throughout all this, Japanese society and Japanese perceptions of the outside world grew steadily more complex. In the previous discussions it was possible, although not always wise, to speak of the experience of a generation. But that sort of generalization is much more difficult for twentieth-century Japan. Divisions between interest groups within Japanese society deepened; even within generalized groupings like business and the armed services, particular interests and foci of competition could produce radically different views of the policies that should be followed. In the Meiji period questions of priority had by no means been lacking, but the diversity of Japanese perceptions of the outside world had to some degree been kept manageable by the evident structure within that world. With the collapse of that structure in the flames of World War I, however, the way was opened for varying perceptions, and Japan's new stature made those perceptions much more important than they had ever been before.

Two developments were of particular importance. One was the interplay of Japanese and Chinese nationalism in the years after World War I, a process that had destructive effects for political stability on both sides of the China Sea. The other was the rise of totalitarian governments in Europe, a development that led segments of the Japanese elite to revise their hierarchy of international prestige and power. In the 1920's Japan gave up its long-standing association with Great Britain to enter the Washington Conference system of pacts, and in the 1930's it gradually abandoned those to enter an alliance with Germany and Italy. Like its new allies, Japan went to war to gain regional hegemony. Instead it experienced defeat and reconstruction.

These political and diplomatic shifts were accompanied by important and as yet inadequately studied changes in perceptions of what individual and national priorities in cultural values should be. In one sense these were a maturation of doubts that Sugita Gempaku had encountered when he first opposed Western practicality and accuracy to Chinese learning. Japanese nativist thought had then posited a purified national essence which justified the turn from

China to the West in defense of the heart of the national tradition. Kume's generation, after experiencing the full flood of Western influence, had witnessed the construction of an official ideology centered around a Confucian-Japanese amalgam of normative values that was supposed to shield Japanese civilization from the destructive aspects of imported materialism and individualism. In the twentieth century all this resulted in a profound ambivalence that was rooted in contradictory attempts to assert the superiority of the indigenous, to strengthen the tradition through the imports, and ultimately to defeat imperialism through imperialism. Many intellectuals and academicians, when confronted with the distasteful alternatives of resisting or reinforcing the sacred myths of nationality, took refuge instead in a privatized, non-political world of specialization. For others, World War II seemed to offer a resolution to paradoxes that had long troubled them, but they only deepened their quandary by a wistful slogan, calling on their countrymen to "overcome modernity," by which they meant non-Japanese materialism. They were overcome by that modernity instead, but the echoes of their assertions remain to complicate the cacophony of Japan's industrial civilization in the 1970's.

It would require many times the space available to do justice to these themes. I shall content myself with examining some aspects of the interwar and war years to see what light they shed on the world view of Japan in our own day. Let me begin with some observations on the interwar period.

1. *Between the Wars*

The principal divisions that developed in the
first third of the twentieth century were those between
the Meiji generation and those who criticized their
perception of the world as out of date. The Meiji men
had seen their country come to greatness under the
shadow of the British fleet, and they had little doubt
that Japan's future could best be guaranteed by keeping as its first priority the friendship of the major
maritime powers. One of the most cogent statements
of this view can be found in the memoirs of the late
Prime Minister Yoshida, a crusty Anglophile who saw
it his mission to restore Japan's close working arrangements with England and America in the years
after World War II. As he saw it, Japan had prospered
as long as it kept those priorities clear, and it met disaster when it did not. But even he granted that there
had been problems about maintaining this course after
the Meiji period ended in1912. One was that some
Japanese felt that the Anglo-Japanese alliance limited
their options in terms of new opportunities presented
by the collapse of Imperial China. More generally,
the end of empire in Turkey, Russia, and Germany in
World War I made it difficult to speak of following
policies predicated upon those empires. How could
one be faithful to the status quo when the status quo
had disappeared?

Another problem was the development of what Professor Iriye has called the competing expansionism of
the United States. The growing distrust between the
United States and Japan, particularly after the

Twenty-One Demands of 1915, made the English nervous about their ties with Japan, and how could Japan have confidence in an alliance with a reluctant partner? At Washington in 1922 and particularly at London in 1930 there seemed to be clear evidence of an Anglo-American lineup against Japan. For many Japanese it seemed that race and culture were the ultimate determinants; the arguments about racial equality at Versailles, and the American immigration legislation of 1924, showed what Japan was up against. Even the Meiji leaders had become increasingly alarmed about racial policies in the early years of the twentieth century. During the Russo-Japanese War Japan had gone to great lengths to avoid any appearance of taking on an Asian role, and earlier efforts to avoid the stigma of the word "Asia" (as with Fukuzawa's famous essay) had shown the same concern. But if such efforts failed, and if the promises of Western cooperation were to be subject to other priorities that Japan could not affect, then a strong Japan might well reconsider its stance and strike out for regional dominance.

This, at any rate, was the view of important sectors of the army. There were moves in this direction as early as World War I, when some of the Meiji army men thought seriously about stronger ties with Germany, a rejection of the English alliance, and a stronger presence on the Asian continent. The experience of World War I, which the Japanese watched from a safe distance, also convinced many army planners that in the new round of international competition Japan would face new requirements; victory would go to those who were prepared with integrated and planned economies. If the resources of the world were to be dominated by Western imperialists, who would deny them to Japan, then Japan should prepare to take things into its own hands. This view was worked out in detail by General Ishiwara Kanji, a brilliant but erratic student of war who developed a theory of world conflict for his lectures at the War College in Tokyo. Ishiwara predicted that technological progress would bring a struggle for regional dominance and ultimately for world leadership. The utilization of technology would require central state planning on an even larger scale than that begun in wartime Germany. In the final stages, air power, symbolized by planes able to circle the globe without refueling, would bring victory and world unification. The final struggle would be between the United States, the leader of Western civilization, and Japan, the leader of Asia. In preparation for this Japan would have to develop state management of industry, a military dictatorship, and a mass party. It should begin by consolidating its control of the natural and human resources of northeast Asia. Step one would be the seizure of Manchuria, followed by the incorporation of north China and eastern Siberia; then could follow the construction of the industrial empire necessary for the final showdown with the United States.

In 1931 Ishiwara, then Staff Officer of the Kwantung Army, was able to implement the first step of his theory by helping to stage the Manchurian Incident. But thereafter everything went badly for him. He did not approve of the clumsy arrangements of the new puppet state, and felt that psychological and political opportunities were wasted by Japan's disregard of Chinese nationalism. In 1937 Ishiwara, now in a high post in the General Staff, did his best to prevent the China incident from expanding into war because he was convinced that Japan's planning and consolidation were at too primitive a stage to risk larger hostilities. Thereafter he fell out with General Tōjō Hideki, denounced him in some startling acts of insubordination, and ended in early retirement. This premature exit from leadership positions probably spared Ishiwara trial as a major war criminal. After the war he experimented with a rural commune movement that would, he hoped, point to a future "Asian" role for a Japan that could still be remade in its own image rather than in those of Harry Truman or Joseph Stalin. To the last he was a spokesman for a distinctive identity for Japan.

Of course there were many degrees between Yoshida's Anglophile position and Ishiwara's exuberant apocalyptic stance, but their ideas provided the poles of the argument. Opinion within the military establishment itself was deeply divided on issues of priorities and possibilities. Factionalism rooted in personal and regional antagonisms was inevitable in armed services that had not known the challenge of performance against an enemy since the Meiji wars, and it was worsened by generational cleavages. Radicalism had at one extreme groups of young officers with an almost nihilistic contempt for the establishment they served, convinced that their fervor, and the commitment of action in violence that would hasten basic changes within the Japanese polity, were all that counted. Smaller groups of higher ranking officers admired that intensity, moderated its extremes, and also counted on it to further their own cause at headquarters. Innovative reformers disparaged all such heroics and emphasized the importance of modernizing the military establishment in equipment and organization. To the radicals such modernization seemed a reliance on materialistic means and a spiritual surrender to the Western world. Their priorities were for struggle against all materialism, especially that of the resurgent Soviet Union, and for that struggle they advocated the spirit of the "Imperial Army," or *Kōgun*. Thus the military was torn by dissension and insubordination rooted in fanaticism. The ability of the high command, at the emperor's insistence, to crush a revolt in Tokyo in 1936, together with the capability Soviet forces showed to curb Japanese adventurism at the Manchurian-Siberian borders in 1938 and 1939, combined to prevent this turbulent maelstrom from disintegrating in a shower of fiery fragments.

The events of the 1930's brought a mix of terror and repression at home, aggression abroad, rising criticism from overseas, and a tendency to close ranks in the face of that repression and criticism. There was an often paranoid reaction to resistance and resentment in China, genuine fear of communist advances on the mainland, and a corrosive decline of confidence in the possibilities of international cooperation under the pressures of depression and of economic nationalism.

It would be a formidable assignment to try to

schematize Japan's world view in those years. The noisy affirmation of Japanese superiority was difficult to refute in public, and this helped to muffle many doubts. Undoubtedly political moderates and most of the business establishment continued to keep their eyes on the Anglo-American side, with its international prestige and trade balances. Yet even the most committed of them were seriously handicapped by the evidence of anti-Japanese feeling and policy. Nitobe Inazō, an American-educated scientist, educator, and Quaker who had devoted most of his career to being a "bridge across the Pacific" by educating Americans about Japan and Japanese about the United States, had been so outraged by the immigration act of 1924, with its exclusion of Japanese, that he vowed not to visit the United States again until its repeal, but as tempers shortened in 1931 he broke his pledge for a final trip to reassure Americans about his country's basic political health. His own health failed first, and he died before completing his mission. This desperate and futile measure somehow symbolized failures of communication within Japanese society and between Japan and the outside world, for few Japanese, whatever their views of army intransigence, doubted their country's special place and rights in Manchuria, or saw much difference between that and the United States' assumption of a special role in Latin America.

There were also advocates of planning who saw in the fascist states of Europe the evidence of a new and possibly decisive trend in international affairs. Europe's leaders, they pointed out, and especially the Germans, whose state structure and philosophy had provided such important models for the Meiji establishment, had found it necessary to reject the individualism and materialism of democratic institutions. Japan too should reform its state structure, for capitalism and representative institutions had worked poorly and had heightened divisions within society. Japan had at hand a family system bolstered by laws which granted family heads authority over their family members. These microcosmic pyramids should reach up to the national hierarchy headed by the divine emperor-father. The result would be a purified structure free of self-assertion and self-will and perfectly united in national service and devotion. The emphases on race and state that came from distant Europe thus served to encourage assertions of priority for the superior Japanese polity of "family state." The weakness and divisions of the West's democratic states, and the dissatisfactions of their colonies in Asia, held both lessons and opportunities for Japan. Intellectuals struggled to find significance for Japan's mission as a struggle by Asia against imperialism, and ideologists and critics cautiously greeted the new turn of direction as a struggle to "overcome modernity."

Thus for many reasons the consensus on a hierarchy of nations that Japan had worked out in the Meiji years disintegrated, and with it Japan's internal stability. The world looked very different to army and to navy leaders, to businessmen, and to other groups. No part of it looked more different than China, which was struggling toward a new national military leadership headed by Chiang Kai-shek. Japanese comment about modern China tended to overlook its problems and achievements and to concentrate on its weakness and shortcomings. "Asian leadership" meant Japanese leadership, for little was to be expected from its larger neighbor. Chinese disorder also contained dangers of communist infection. It was in fact the extension of Kuomintang rule to Manchuria that helped to provide the spark for the Manchurian Incident. In the Meiji period a young Japan had had its doubts about an old China, but in the years between the wars a young China—young in terms of political leadership and political ideas—alarmed an older Japan.

As he looked back on this scene shortly before his death, Mr. Yoshida contrasted the turbulence of his day with the relative unanimity of the Meiji Period, when there had been substantial agreement on the structure of international society and the requirements for Japanese affiliation. "What strikes me about those [Meiji] events," he wrote, "is the unanimity with which the Japanese Government and people generally acted in those days, in contrast to the dissensions concerning the attitude to be taken towards Great Britain and the United States which were at a later date to mar our politics and policies." Of course Yoshida went on to extend the contrast to the 1950's, when he took the lead in forming the alliance with the United States. As he put it, "The Anglo-Japanese alliance was welcomed by Government and people alike and no one viewed that document as meaning that Japan was truckling to British imperialism or in any danger of becoming a glorified British colony." In 1960, when those words were written, Yoshida's countrymen were deeply divided on the wisdom of the tie with America,

but the events of the 1970's have, I think, served to
vindicate the old man's judgment of his country's ability to combine independence with alliance.

2. The War Decisions

From what has been said, it will be understood
that the decisions that sent the modern Japanese state
careening to war, defeat, and destruction resulted less
from a fundamental restructuring of the international
hierarchy than from the failure to work out a new lad-
der of prestige satisfactorily. Contradictions and con-
fusion led to a series of decisions based more on tactics
than on strategy. Despite all the rhetoric of decisive-
ness, a study of the minutes of the conferences that
produced the decisions for war shows chiefly short-
range planning and wishful thinking about what
would follow the initial victories. China would surely
compromise once more, or else surrender after its
government was crushed by a massive blow. The
United States could surely be held at bay until the
construction of defense lines so strong that the Pacific
would be left to Japan, since America's priorities must
lie in the West. In Europe the imminence of German
victory seemed to put urgency behind a Japanese effort
lest the opportunity for gain in Southeast Asia should
be lost forever. The Russians might provide their good
offices at the last, as the United States had given its
help in 1905.

This whole process still lacks an adequate account,
but what we have leaves little doubt of the hesitation,

the uncertainty, and sometimes the irresponsibility that pervaded the meetings of the decision-makers. They were cheered by the reminders that things had always worked out for the best in previous crises of the modern Japanese state. Each decision they made seemed provisional to them, but it led to a second, and then a third, until the final and total commitment seemed inescapable.

The failures began with China, and it can be maintained that they derived from the inability to work out a coherent world view that had provision for modern Chinese nationalism. Instead, the expressions of that nationalism were all too quickly seen as perversely anti-Japanese. Japanese of many persuasions had come to accept the necessity for a special position on the Chinese mainland. How else could Japan be a great power, with access to the sort of resources the other powers controlled? Complementary vibrations of Chinese and Japanese nationalisms gradually resulted in irreversible oscillations as the two came into head-on collision despite the presence on both sides of those who tried to prevent this from taking place. I have been freshly convinced of this as I read the memoirs of the head of the Shanghai branch of the Japanese news agency. Matsumoto Shigeharu, whom many of us know today as the Chairman of the International House of Japan in Tokyo, describes a series of desperate efforts to get Japanese and Chinese officials to talk to each other. They were efforts in which he and others played honorable roles, but they were doomed to result in nothing more lasting than Japan's relations with the short-lived shadow government of

Wang Ching-wei in Nanking. Far from destroying Chiang Kai-shek, Japan made a national hero of him by its policies, only to cripple his government in the long and bitter conflict that began in 1937.

The China failure led to Japan's clash with the United States, for American efforts to force restraint upon Japan instead drove the Japanese to attack. The stakes and the uncertainties of the gamble pervade the accounts of the councils that made the decision for war. The effort that was being made might not work, but the opportunity to try it would not come a second time, and the alternative was permanent second-class status among the nations. As Admiral Nagano put it, "The government has decided that if there is no war, the fate of the nation is sealed. Even if there is war, the country may be ruined. Nevertheless, a nation that does not fight in this plight has lost its spirit and is already doomed." The "plight" of which he spoke was in part a dwindling supply of oil that could only be replenished by seizure of more while Japan could still fuel its forces. The admiral's words are certainly not those of someone confident in his picture of a new world order. Instead, as he phrased it, the costs of inaction were higher than those of action. It is incidentally ironic to note that the stockpile that then seemed adequate for the initial military phases of the effort would last Japan only a few days at present levels of peacetime use.

But there was something more that pervaded the councils of those days and helped to impel the spokesmen to desperate deeds. In the flood of writing about world affairs of those days, and these, in Japan one finds increasing mention of *jisei*, the mood of the times, or *taisei*, the prevailing current. Increasingly it is suggested that with the exception of the handful of zealots who set out to do something about it, Japanese leaders are usually like the subjects of Japanese novels, people who respond to a flow of events which is basically beyond their control. The times determine what is possible; the wise accept this and do not try to set them right. There is an eloquent statement of this view from Prince Saionji, the last of the Meiji senior statesmen, at the time of the Manchurian Incident:

"The government is just being dragged along by the army, and the situation is indeed distressing, but there is no use in saying, 'How terrible!' or 'Whatever shall I do!' This is probably one phenomenon of a transitional period. If one could only feel that this was indeed the time to put forth one's maximum effort one might even find it an interesting period. But for a statesman to say all the time 'This is a crisis!' or 'I'm at my wit's end!' shows that he does not really understand things. . . ."

It seems to me that this goes beyond an injunction to remain calm. It involves an acceptance of the tide of affairs and serves as a reminder that there are some things one cannot do anything about.

Some Japanese writers suggest that one should relate the psychology of this to the way Japanese speakers use the verb *naru*, to come about, in preference to *tsukuru* or *suru*, to make or to do. The result, they point out, is that things seem to take shape without reference to actors who make them so. One Japanese scholar uses the example of his university faculty in Tokyo. If its minutes are phrased with active verbs, he writes, they are indignantly rejected; they should not read *kō shimashita* (we did thus and so), but they ought to seem to drift, as in *kō narimashita* (things came about in this manner). And while the process of decision-making may be obscure, the conclusion is rather irrevocable; since no one did it, it can hardly be undone.

These flurries with sociolinguistics are lots of fun, but they are also full of pitfalls for the unwary. Most universities' faculty minutes are full of passive verbs, including my own. Modern Japanese history has enough examples of intense and impulsive reaction, even overreaction, to events to make one cautious. But there is something here nonetheless that helps to illumine the strangely passive air that seems to pervade the meetings of decision-makers in 1941. The majority accepted the *jisei* as something given, and the few who sensed disaster tried to modify that *jisei*, or at least their colleagues' perceptions of it, rather than to struggle against their proposed response.

3. *The Japanese Recovery*

The Japanese surrender of 1945 introduced a radically different *jisei* or *taisei*. With Japan at first prostrate and then only gradually able to direct its own affairs, it did not require conscious decision or foresight to accept the fact of American domination of Japanese affairs. Many dates might be suggested for formal and actual return of sovereignty; 1952, with the Treaty of Peace; 1954-1955, when the economy for the first time exceeded prewar performance; 1958, when the First Defense Plan was worked out by Japanese planners; the economic growth of the 1960's, or even 1972, when Prime Minister Satō hailed the reversion of Okinawa as the end of the postwar era. Yet it would be wrong to see all of this period as one of Japanese drift and acceptance of the inevitable, for there is no doubt that Mr. Yoshida and his associates were convinced that their country should seek to associate itself with the trading countries of the West. Japan's leaders clearly made conscious decisions about minimal defense forces and reliance upon an American alliance, and they worked skillfully to sidetrack the urging of John Foster Dulles and others who belatedly thought Japan should do more and rearm more rapidly. The steps of their decisions are often hard to document, and they are in fact becoming apparent only now, as government documents for that period are declassified. Indeed, some of the flurry of surprise that was evoked by the award of the Nobel Prize for Peace to Mr. Satō in 1974 suggests that it may be almost as difficult to assign individual responsibility for Japan's cautious course since the war as it was for the Tokyo Tribunal to assign individual blame for Japanese aggression a quarter century earlier.

Nevertheless it was clearly a changed *jisei* that helped to channel the Japanese response. In a postwar world dominated by two superpowers, Japan was fortunate to be occupied by one and not by both. The victory of communism in China and the political posture of India made it natural that Japan, with all its latent industrial capacity, should become steadily more important to the United States. Strategically also, Japan was essential to the United Nations effort in Korea, and it remained essential to the American security stance in Asia. In turn Japan helped to stabilize the Western Pacific by its own stability and growth and emerged as a real partner in what began as a very unequal alliance, one dominated by the American partner.

The dimensions of American assistance to Japan went far beyond the highly visible forms of aid and protection. Japanese purchases of American technology helped to fuel the fires of the new industrial revolution that brought Japan its startling economic growth. The free trade era and the inexpensive raw materials of the 1950's and 1960's rendered obsolete the arguments for autarchy and empire that had carried such weight in the 1930's, and the collapse of western empires in Asia brought Japan ready access to resources in Southeast Asia that had been the immediate objects of the Pacific War. A Japan starved for consumer goods developed a vast domestic market that put an end to prewar theories of Japanese dependence upon exports to balance the impoverishment of its own population. American sponsorship of Japanese membership in international organizations helped to ease Japanese access to foreign markets. Meanwhile Japan's trading relationship with the United States mushroomed into a $30 billion two-way trade, the largest exchange in history between overseas countries. Even if contiguous states are included, Japanese-American trade was exceeded only by American trade with Canada. Japan became and remains America's largest market for agricultural products in a trade that takes almost one-fifth of the United States' total agricultural export. Today there is more acreage in the United States producing food products for Japan than there is in Japan itself. In addition to agricultural goods, Japan is a major market for manufactured goods and industrial raw materials. As Frank Gibney recently put it, Japan's is the other big consumer economy in the world after our own. Largely in consequence of this, United States trade with Asian countries exceeded that with Europe for the first time in 1977.

In the other direction came the growing tide of Japanese manufactures to the United States, a flow that grew steadily in quality and quantity. Although other markets also opened to Japan and although the proportion of Japanese manufactures absorbed by American purchases diminished over time, the enormous importance of the American market remains obvious.

Throughout this period, the decision by the United States that the defense of Japan was vital to the interest of the United States made impressive savings possible for Japan. These began with American insistence on Article 9 in the postwar Japanese constitution. While the exact authorship and final responsibility for the idealistic renunciation of war as an instrument of policy remain somewhat obscurely divided between General MacArthur and Prime Minister Shidehara, there is no doubt today that MacArthur favored that disarmament strongly, that he refused to moderate his stand even after his government wanted him to do so in 1948, and that he agreed fully with Prime Minister Yoshida in resisting efforts to get Japan to speed the pace of its rearmament after the outbreak of the Korean War. There is also no doubt, however, that Article 9 reflected the overwhelming sentiments of the Japanese people at the time it was adopted, and that that support, loudly articulated from many quarters, made it impossible for the conservative leaders to change it by the time they thought about doing so in the 1950's.

The *jisei*, in other words, did indeed change powerfully and decisively, but the Japanese response was also skillful, purposeful, and eminently rational. Japanese leaders resisted rapid rearmament on American terms lest it lock them into American strategy and alienate their Asian neighbors. By the time they could contemplate moves more nearly under their own direction and more in line with the dignity and power they felt their national power required, shrinking electoral margins made such plans more difficult.

The *jisei* within Japan was changing rapidly as well, and set new boundaries for what was possible and wise. The new education and freedom were producing a society with a far less pronounced sense of hierarchy. If there was less hierarchy at home, there was also less point in attempting to rank other countries within an orderly rank of eminence. By the 1970's the outside world was treating Japan with more respect and even admiration than ever before, and reminders of inferiority and second-class membership in the world order were few. Japan's society was as well run, or better, its life as good or better, and its goods as good or better than those of any other country. Indeed, a recent author suggests, Japan may be "Number One," with lessons for America.

One result was a consciousness of modernity that transcended politics. As the age groups that had experienced the worst hardships of war, destruction, and reconstruction began to have younger contemporaries join them, the notes of deprivation and weakness that characterized commentary in the 1950's began to change. In time these changes affected the political discourse of even those who had hoped to ride that poverty and despair to power. In the summer of 1974 I heard an election speech by the communist leader Nozaka Sanzō. He assured his audience that although conservatives talked as though Japanese communists would carry out repressive policies of the sort that Russia and China had experienced, the Japanese Communist Party had no such intent. There was no need for repression. Russia and China had been underdeveloped and backward countries, and their governments had had to take strong measures. But Japan was modernized, and its society had passed the point where coercion was necessary. What was needed was social legislation. And with that Nozaka went on to discuss day care centers, inflation, and protection of the environment.

The new Japan also became more internationally experienced than before. Japan remains parochial and insular in important respects, and the unique quality of Japanese culture combines with the limiting nature of the Japanese language to enfold the Japanese in a consciousness of social nationality that may have no parallel elsewhere. Nevertheless it operates within a context of greater awareness of the outside world than ever existed before. The war years saw millions of Japanese go overseas, while Occupation duty and the Korean war brought millions of foreigners, most of them Americans, to Japan. Much more important, I suspect, was the large-scale movement of young Japanese overseas as students. Fulbright, private programs, and enterprises sent thousands of students and employees out of the country in a tide that continues today. And then, in the 1960's, Japanese started to travel abroad. In 1969 the Japanese who went abroad for the first time exceeded the number of foreigners who came to Japan. That year 710,000 Japanese went abroad. In 1974 the number rose to 2,340,000; in 1977 it was 3,151,431. The vast majority are young men and women in their twenties and thirties. Even if a good number of these travellers move in the insulation of a peer-group tour, the cumulative impact of their experience has to be significant. In prewar years there were significant groups of Japanese immigrants abroad, but very few individual expatriates. Today, for the first time in history, there are also large numbers of Japanese living alone abroad; they are painting in Paris, playing in all major orchestras, and teaching Japanese in places that never expected to have to meet a demand for such language instruction. Even Japanese radicalism has gone international. It no longer restricts itself to attacks on Japanese businessmen and politicians, but makes a cause as distant as Palestinian nationalism its own.

). Changes in Japanese commerce: Deshima, the Nagasaki trading station or ıe Netherlands East India Company, in 1804.

1. Hommoku wharf of the Nissan Motor Company, 1978.

4. *Toward Definition of a Role*

Throughout the decades of recovery and reconstruction, leadership in Japan lay with a generation that received its lower education in the Meiji era, and the adult population had been tempered by the frustrations and hardships of the 1930's and 1940's. The Japanese were deeply divided politically between conservative and socialist camps whose spokesmen held radically differing views on world problems, and both sets of views were rooted in attitudes and convictions formed in earlier days. Gradually a new and middle consensus began to form. By the mid 1970's over one-half of the Japanese population had been born after the war, with only slight and diminishing personal experience of the hardships to which it led, and none at all of the disastrous adventurism that brought it about. The extremes of generational experience are nowhere more pronounced than in Japan, and they too affect the restless search for meaning that pervades much contemporary commentary.

In the early 1970's Japan's steady progress toward economic growth, economic affluence, and the international exposure of the 1960's met rude shocks which produced an outburst of speculation within Japan on the possibilities for Japan and the Japanese in the modern world. A flood of introspective writing focusing on what was unique and important about Japan—called *Nihonron*—began to pour off the presses. In contrast to the Japanism of the late nineteenth century, which tended to be assertive and attempted to be definitive, this literature is questioning and speculative, but it represents some of the same psychological needs and drives.

The crises that broke into the orderly world of the 1960's do not require detailed description. The "Nixon shocks" found the United States expressing impatience with Japan's reluctance to heed American warnings, by the application of shock treatment on issues of currency revaluation, textile quotas, and import levies. The sudden American turn toward normalization of relations with mainland China caught the Japanese off guard and seemed to imply inconstancy on the part of Japan's major ally; lack of American consultation seemed to imply distrust of Japan and possible reversal of America's entire security stance. Since this coincided in time with the United States failure in Southeast Asia and suggested a larger disengagement, there were those who ruminated on Great Britain's dwindling enthusiasm for the Anglo-Japanese alliance a half century earlier.

On top of this, the oil crisis of 1973 brought home the vulnerability of all the industrialized states, and, most particularly, of Japan. Japan became acutely aware of the fact that it lacked not only oil but all other natural resources, and even food. A brief and unwise American ban on soy beans, in which Japan was 92 percent dependent upon American sources, underscored the specific as well as general malaise.

In addition, the oil shock came at a time when the theretofore unquestioned consensus on growth had been weakened by popular awareness of the costs of crash programs of industrial expansion in terms of environmental degradation. On every hand the evidence of damage to the environment and the sudden growth of voluntary citizens' associations to protest new factories, new roads, new airports, new rail lines, and new power plants reflected the change in outlook. Japan's GNP in 1977 was third in the world, one-third that of the United States and only slightly below that of the U.S.S.R., slightly more than those of France and England combined, and over eight times that of all of Southeast Asia. In per capita terms Japan stood about tenth, if the oil-producing countries are passed over and Benelux and Scandinavia are treated as units. But if national product is measured on an area basis, Japan's GNP is five times as intensive as that of the United States. If the unit of measurement is changed to arable land, Japan's is twelve times that of the United States. There has been more crowding, more pollution, and more monoxide than any other population has had to experience. What made it possible to endure was the extraordinary integration, discipline, and dignity that characterizes Japanese society. But some sort of limit was being reached. Popular resistance to the development of much needed alternative sources of energy through nuclear power plants revealed additional sources of psychological repugnance. Growth alone was no longer unquestioned as a goal.

As the price of oil spiraled upwards, Japan's economy was plunged into the world recession that all the industrial countries experienced, but its response was made more sluggish because of the government's reluctance to bring on a new inflation at a time when levels were already high. Since domestic inventories were also high, and since patterns of permanent employment and underfinanced industries made it difficult to cut production drastically, Japanese goods flowed abroad in constantly greater amounts. Washington allowed the yen to appreciate against the dollar, in the expectation that more expensive imports would become less competitive, but this proved a very slow process. Instead, the dollar imbalance continued to grow because the imports were also more expensive, while Japan's dollar accumulations made its raw material import costs less onerous. Within five puzzling years the fragility that had seemed to characterize the Japanese economy in American eyes had given way to record trade surpluses. Japanese exports throughout the 1970's grew at astounding rates, one-quarter of them coming to the United States, while the American share of imports to Japan declined from 30 percent (in 1970) to 18 percent (in 1977). American criticism focused on Japan's contribution to the American trade deficit and on its failure to contribute to efforts to maintain the health of the system of free trade, while the Japanese countered with comments on America's inability to moderate its own need for imported energy. The specific trade differences were papered over in a series of agreements that eased the sense of crisis, most recently in 1979, but they remained unsolved. As the Japanese economy grew and as the Japanese-American relationship became more complex, they seemed to increase in scale. A decade ago the issues were over textiles; then steel, and, soon, perhaps, computers. Japan was no longer a follower. The islands that were targets for Boeing aircraft and Kaiser ships now fabricate parts for Boeing and negotiate for purchase of Kaiser steel plants.

One could easily spend a great deal of time on each of the factors I have raised, for they are extremely complex and important. I suggest them chiefly to make the point that the world *jisei* to which Japan responds has been in such rapid and drastic change that it is dangerous to try to make predictions. It is instructive to check back through recent decades to see how often even well-informed commentary on Japan has had to shift to accommodate itself to changes no one had foreseen. One found in successive decades judgments that Japan's economic predicament was virtually incapable of solution; that (by the 1950's) things looked better, but still gloomy; in the 1960's futurologists suddenly hailed the future as Japan's and saw its patterns as providing meaning for the rest of us. The oil crisis brought a sudden round of farewells to economic growth and greatness for Japan, and today, a mere half decade later, Japanese ships loaded with the product of well-paid, hard-working Japanese crowd the world's ports more than ever before. Through all of this the Japanese have responded practically, unemotionally, and quietly to opportunity as they saw it, avoiding fanfare and the limelight and protesting that their options are really very limited.

We should not overlook the logic of what they say. In the new *jisei* Japan's place in the international order does indeed make it peculiarly dependent on the rest of the world. Its dependence upon imports finds Japan the world's largest importer in commodity after commodity, with the exception of oil, where America leads. Japan's oil imports make up over 80 percent of its energy needs; it also imports 60 percent of the coal it uses. Imported oil is the basis for almost everything Japan produces and not, as in the United States, preponderately used for domestic consumption. In 1972 Japan's oil consumption was 10 percent of the world total, or 300 million kiloliters. Until the oil crises there was talk of having this consumption triple every five or six years, and some prophets predicted a line of super-tankers spaced a few nautical miles apart all the way from the Persian Gulf to Tokyo Bay. Small wonder that the Arab-Israeli war of 1973 and the oil shock that followed produced such a sharp sense of crisis.

If one adds to this the requirements of international markets for Japanese goods, it is no surprise that Japan is more internationally oriented than ever before, that more Japanese go and are abroad than ever before, and that ideas of regional self-sufficiency or mastery are few in Japan today. They made some sense in the 1930's; much of Asia was dominated by colonial powers, economic nationalism made it difficult to increase markets abroad, and the supply of raw materials required was still sufficiently finite to encourage planners like General Ishiwara to think they could do something about it. In today's *jisei* a policy of regional autarchy makes no sense at all.

The world order has changed just as much, and the final contours of that change are not in sight. The era of national empires gave way to the dominance of the super-powers, and that to the more nearly multipolar world in which we live. Now even super-powers find themselves with sharply limited alternatives, and the producer powers, symbolized by OPEC, have discovered that they too have leverage. The powerful need the weak.

Perhaps most important of all, there are no longer model states for Japan. The United States no doubt still tops the list in importance and visibility for Japan, but the limitations of its power and wisdom have been shown by a range of ills from Viet Nam and Watergate to the more recent recession. Europe remains a focus of travel and culture for Japan, but hardly the object of institutional borrowing that it once was.

The changes in Japanese perceptions of China are perhaps the most interesting of all. To some degree, as I have suggested, the Japanese in earlier years defined themselves in terms of China; first negatively, in terms of a cultural ideal, and then more positively, in terms of Japan's modernization. For some years after World War II, Mao's China became once again a focus of admiration, this time for the Japanese Left. Familiarity with the new China gradually convinced increasing numbers of Japanese of the great and growing cultural and institutional gulf between them and their continental neighbor, and the irrationality of the disastrous Cultural Revolution disillusioned all but the most devoted China watchers. Nevertheless, Japanese of many persuasions felt themselves shackled by American policies with respect to Taiwan and Peking, and feared isolation from their powerful neighbor. China policy, related as it was to the American Security Treaty, was long among the most divisive issues in Japanese domestic politics.

The Nixon-Kissinger turn to Peking buried the old China policy without fanfare. Prime Minister Tanaka rushed to Peking in his turn, and went farther than Mr. Nixon by reversing Japan's relations between Taiwan and Peking at one stroke. For all the Japanese resentment of the lack of consultation in the American turn to China, I think it is probably true that the Japanese government was the most immediate beneficiary of the American moves. China suddenly ceased to be a divisive issue in Japanese politics. Similarly, in 1978 Mr. Brzezinski's trip to Peking to continue American discussions toward normalization with the People's Republic was followed by a visit by Japan's Foreign Minister to work out details of the Treaty of Amity between Japan and China that was signed in 1978. With that the last remnants of the hostility of the 1930's were laid to rest. That same year a long-term trade agreement provided the prospect of extensive imports of Chinese coal and oil in exchange for Japanese manufactures. There has been an extensive flow of Japanese travellers and businessmen to the People's Republic, and Japan ranks first among China's trading partners. Few expect the Chinese trade to eclipse Japan's commerce with the industrialized countries. On the other hand, the economic and political importance of the China ties will make the Japanese very cautious about increasing their commitments to the Soviet Union, especially so long as the Russians remain inflexible on the issue of the northern islands that they seized from the Japanese in the closing days of World War II. The combination of fear and dislike that has characterized the Japanese responses to Russia throughout the last century shows little sign of changing.

Equally interesting and difficult is the effort to predict Japan's attitudes toward Southeast and South Asia. Here the task is one of telescoping into a few years lessons about sensitivity to local pride that have required many years to be learned in other countries. Prime Minister Tanaka's reception in Southeast Asia in 1974 was indicative of some of the dimensions of the problem; he received complaints about Japanese arrogance, favoritism, selfishness, and separatism. But on another level the response of the Japanese media to Tanaka's reception was very interesting indeed. With scarcely a word of self-defense, they used the occasion for self-denunciation, self-reflection, and vows to do better. The slow, but real, development of cultural diplomacy, educational assistance, and development assistance promises more forward steps. Prime Minister Fukuda's stance at the Manila meeting of Southeast Asian states in 1977 showed the beginnings of a new and more responsible stance in that area.

One might conclude by asking what parameters to Japanese decision possibilities will be set by the international environment of the immediate future. What are the considerations that any government concerned with the livelihood and well-being of 116 million Japanese must take into account?

Surely the first of these remains the importance of Japan's relationship with the United States. It is a relationship whose economic importance I have already mentioned. The two countries basically share the same interest in a large and expanding world trade providing consumer goods for free economies. A relationship so large and many-sided produces unparalleled provision for friction as well as for cooperation, and the cultural and linguistic gaps that separate the two countries will continue to bedevil efforts to work out solutions to the problems that arise. Within Japan, however, social change is operating to reduce the drag of institutions like an antiquated distribution system and an outdated electoral system that combine to set up roadblocks against efforts to increase Japanese imports, although in the meanwhile specific centers of unemployment and distress in the United States can resonate with lingering resentment of the success of Japanese goods. Yet in the long run consumer interests in both urban markets will operate to lessen some of these frictions, though others will arise. In the meantime it is the heavy responsibility of political leaders and popular media to keep those frictions in the perspective of the larger and more astounding success that Japanese-American relations have become.

In security terms, again, the Japanese and American interest is identical. Japan's long fear that the American tie might separate it from the colossus on the mainland has been vitiated by Peking's shift to see that tie as a welcome restraint on the Soviet Union, and as a result the contentious wrangles of Japanese politics have been replaced by a gradual consensus on the values of both American bases and Japanese defense forces. As a result the long-standing decline in election majorities for the governing Liberal-Democratic Party has less significance for Japanese foreign and security policies than once seemed probable, since the conservatives are not likely to have difficulty finding enough like-minded opponents to work out a coalition government if they should find it necessary to do so.

There are other and important aspects of the Japanese-American relationship that will not fade. Japan's representative government and larger institutional patterns that were created in the course of the postwar reforms created important areas of shared experience, and periodic suggestions by commentators of imminent change for that pattern have gradually declined as the durability of and popular support for those institutions have become accepted facts of political life in Japan.

In view of growing sensitivity and national self-consciousness on the part of Japan's new generations, however, a degree of disengagement from the U.S. tie is probably a condition for its retention. The United States has done its share toward making this easy through the Nixon shocks, the soy-bean issue, and an occasional scolding tone in trade negotiations, while the Japanese government and media do their share by stubborn resistance to American calls for Japanese moderation in exports and for acceleration of imports. Japan's relations with the Peoples' Republic of China provide new and inportant opportunities for maneuverability and autonomy, and its dominant position in the economies of others of its neighbors adds to this. Most recently, the changing nature of the international oil market begins to make an independent stance on energy possible. None of this provides a viable alternative to the close relationship with the

United States, with its dimensions of security, commerce, and institutional structure, but taken together these new relationships remove the feelings of isolation and followership that provided such rich soil for self-doubt and frustration in Japanese commentary throughout the 1950's and 1960's.

Thus it seems to me that the options for genuine innovation and realignment for Japan are very limited. For two decades now, writers have been telling us that an era was about to come to an end in Japan. The Occupation would end; reconstruction would be accomplished; a reaction against American leadership would set in; nationalist sentiment would flower once again; conservative dominance would end. Implicit in much of this was the assumption that the existing order of forces and priorities was somehow transitional and unnatural, and that sweeping changes were in the offing. Unstated also was an assumption that Japan's restless thrust for eminence and recognition in the last century would require more in the way of status and prominence than had so far been achieved. Japanese nationalism was about to reassert itself.

There are items that can be used to substantiate this. There is much more satisfaction with Japan's new importance than there was. Some nationalistic legislators give occasional indication that a generation less chastened by war and defeat is tired of the caution shown by its elders. The way the Japanese press responds to occasional issues of national prestige can, to some degree, suggest the past. American bases and nuclear carriers continue to be fair game. There are calls for building an armaments industry to lessen reliance on others; a prolonged economic turndown could strengthen arguments for exporting arms. Even China, long so vehement against Japanese rearmament, could urge that rearmament as preferable to continued Japanese reliance upon America. Renewed violence on the Korean peninsula and the emergence of anything resembling a threat to Japan there could produce genuine alarm and perhaps destabilize Japanese politics by encouraging conservatives to call for a greater defense capacity and for their opponents to redouble their demands for a more pacifist and neutral course.

All of which is to say the *jisei* could change. But while a cataclysmic decline in the international economy or incredibly shortsighted policies by political leaders inside and outside Japan could produce a shift, I do not see major changes required by any of Japan's modern history. Japan's hundred-year effort for recognition has been successful. It was preceded by centuries of pacifism under the unlikely leadership of two-sworded samurai. There are roots for moderation as well as for militarism in Japanese history, and the external rewards for militarism at this juncture are few indeed.

Japanese and Japanologists write about Japan's search for a role, with the assumption that it lacks one. My own suggestion is that the Japanese are finding they have had one all along. For years they have seemed to accept this role because they lacked the consensus for an alternative, but in the meantime it has come to assume a reality of its own, and to develop its own consensus. Part of the desire for a role is rooted in the need to work out some form of autonomy and uniqueness. But rearmament and strong arm policies contain nothing new. What is unique in the Japanese case is the fact of a major power, lightly armed, forgoing the forms of outward power that it could easily afford and quickly build, and choosing to pick its way through the minefield instead of trying for a security that would in any case prove illusory and expensive. Such behavior moreover fits the facts of the *jisei* we see. Japan is the only major power that can afford no enemies. It is the only major power not fenced in by a pattern of armament and regional alliance. It has the only major industrial plant that is quite free from reliance upon the provision of military implements for itself and for others. It is the only major power quite unthreatened by its neighbors, all of whom are satisfied powers through recent victory. Its institutions are premised upon the values of democracy and peace, and its surplus can still go to the amelioration of major problems of environment and development that plague both the developed and the underdeveloped world.

For each of the previous discussions, it was possible to focus on an individual whose memoirs in old age described the significance of what he had seen and done in his prime. Sugita Gempaku saw the development of knowledge about the West through books, and Kume Kunitake experienced at first hand the world that Japan had to enter and to emulate. Before long we should be able to identify comparable accounts from among those that are beginning to emerge from the leaders of the postwar era. This is a remarkable generation that rebuilt their country and set it on the course it knows today.

I have already mentioned the case of Matsumoto

Shigeharu, whose memoirs are now available. Consider what he has seen and done. Born in 1899, he graduated from Tokyo University and began his graduate study there until the 1923 earthquake with its destruction of facilities suggested the advisability of study abroad. There followed years in America, at Yale, and in New York, where Charles Beard convinced him that the problem of American-Japanese relations centered on China. The banking crisis of 1927 found Matsumoto in Oxford, whence he was summoned by an uncle whose shipyard was suddenly in trouble. Now came the decision for a career as an "international journalist"; a profession he saw as a fledgling international civil service. Soon Matsumoto was at Tokyo University again to prepare in economics and in American studies. The possibility of a permanent position in American studies there fell victim to the great depression budget cuts. Instead he moved, via Institute of Pacific Relations conferences in Kyoto and Shanghai, to China as head of the Dōmei Press office. Here he had his chance to work on Beard's warning that China policy was what counted. In his Shanghai years Matsumoto participated in efforts to reach an agreement first with Chiang Kai-shek and then Wang Ching-wei. Return to Japan found him a political associate and advisor of Prince Konoe, and ultimately a participant in the moves to bring a hopeless war to an end. Next came Occupation and purge, the practice of law, editing a small journal of opinion, and finally the opportunity to head the International House of Japan. From the time of its opening in 1955 Matsumoto made it his special effort to try to bridge American and

12. Matsumoto Shigeharu.

Japanese China policies, a course that could be realized only in the 1970's.

Mr. Matsumoto's presence has long been a formidable one in Tokyo, and his name has appeared regularly on every list of influential persons. If Kume experienced his country's rise from weakness, Matsumoto and his generation witnessed its destruction and rapid reconstruction. Both men, in their seventies and eighties, could look over the society of their day, a country gaining in strength and increasingly oriented to the world, and say, "I saw this happen. In fact I helped it to happen."

Kume's expectation of a constructive role for his country was dashed almost as he penned his words. The hopes of the postwar moderate leaders rest on firmer grounds, although their compatriots' slowness to translate international experience into truly international consciousness reminds the optimist of the need for caution and constrains him from prediction. Rationality may suggest a given course, but neither men nor nations are always rational. Therefore we would give even more for the future account of someone now approaching his prime in Japan. His story of national developments and international role, of wisdom and of error, would also tell us how our world will go. For the fact of a powerful and influential Japan is one to which America is only beginning to adjust, and the speed and success with which we do this will tell a good deal about the way life is lived and seen on both sides of the Pacific.

BIBLIOGRAPHICAL NOTE

Challenges to the Confucian Order

I have suggested some of the dimensions of the Japanese relationship to China in two essays, "On Cultural Borrowing," in Albert Craig, ed., *Japan: A Comparative View* (Princeton University Press, 1979), and "Japanese Views of China During the Meiji Period," in Albert Feuerwerker, Rhoads Murphey and Mary C. Wright, eds., *Approaches to Modern Chinese History* (University of California Press, 1967). It is a vast subject, on which a great deal remains to be done. The response to Po Chü-i is discussed by Hirakawa Sukehiro in *Yōkyoku no shi to Seiyō no shi* (Tokyo, Asahi, 1975). Donald Keene's appraisal of the 1770's will be found in his *The Japanese Discovery of Europe, 1720-1830* (Stanford: Stanford University Press, 1969), a revised and expanded edition of *The Japanese Discovery of Europe: Honda Toshiaki and other Discoverers, 1720-1798* (1952). I have adapted Sugita's description of the famous dissection from Keene's p. 22 and from the full translation of Sugita's memoirs provided by Eikoh Ma, "The Impact of Western Medicine on Japan. Memoirs of a Pioneer, Sugita Gempaku, 1733-1817," in *Archives Internationales d'Histoire des Sciences* (Paris, June and December 1961). There is also a more recent translation by Ryōzō Matsumoto, edited by Tomio Ogata, issued as *Dawn of Western Science in Japan: Rangaku Kotohajime* (Tokyo, Hokuseido, 1969). Professor Haga's treatment of

Sugita is in Vol. 22 of *Nihon no meichō* (Great Books of Japan), *Sugita Gempaku, Hiraga Gennai, Shiba Kōkan* (Tokyo, Chūō Kōron, 1971), which contains a splendid introduction as well as the texts of the Sugita passages mentioned. Donald Keene's translation of Chikamatsu's drama *The Battles of Coxinga* appears in his *Major Plays of Chikamatsu* (New York: Columbia University Press, 1961), and earlier in *The Battles of Coxinga* (London: Taylor's Foreign Press, 1951). Motoori Norinaga's works are conveniently brought together with an introduction by Ishikawa Jun in *Nihon no meichō*: Vol. 21 (Tokyo, Chūō Kōron, 1970), and Yoshikawa Kōjirō, ed., *Motoori Norinaga shū*, in *Nihon no shisō* (Japanese Thought), Vol. 15 (Tokyo: Chikuma Shobo, 1969), Motoori is also the subject of a study by Shigeru Matsumoto, *Motoori Norinaga, 1730-1801* (Cambridge: Harvard University Press, 1970). I have adapted the translation from *Tamakatsuma* from the unpublished dissertation of Ronald Morse, "The Search for Japan's National Character and Distinctiveness: Yanagita Kunio (1875-1962) and the Folklore Movement" (Princeton University, 1974). My discussion of Shizuki Tadao is indebted to an unpublished dissertation by Tadashi Yoshida, "The *Rangaku* of Shizuki Tadao: The Introduction of Western Science in Tokugawa Japan," Princeton University, 1974. Professor Harootunian's cautions about the use of China as metaphor are in "The Function of China in Tokugawa Thought," forthcoming in Akira Iriye, ed., *China and Japan: Their Mutual Interaction* (Princeton University Press). Kate Wildman Nakai, "The Nationalization of

Confucianism in Tokugawa Japan: The Problem of Sinocentrism," *Harvard Journal of Asiatic Studies* 40:1 (June 1980), 157-199, dates earlier discussions.

Wisdom Sought Throughout the World

G. B. Sansom, *The Western World and Japan* (New York: Alfred Knopf, 1950 and later printings) remains a lucid and authoritative discussion of the many aspects of Western influence in nineteenth-century Japan. Since these lectures were written, the first Tokugawa embassy to the West has received brilliant treatment in Masao Miyoshi, *As We Saw Them: The First Japanese Embassy to the United States (1860)* (Berkeley: University of California Press, 1979), who examines all the travel diaries to study the mind set of the samurai emissaries. In Japanese, principal guides are Osatake Takeki, *Iteki no kuni e* (To the Barbarians' Countries) (Tokyo: Manrikaku, 1929), and Haga Tōru, *Taikun no shisetsu: Bakumatsu Nihonjin no Seiō taiken* (The Shogun's Missions: the Experience of Late Tokugawa Japanese in the West) (Tokyo: Chūō Kōron, 1968). Vice-ambassador Muragaki's diary, *Kōkai nikki*, was translated by Helen Uno as *Kokai Nikki: The Diary of the First Japanese Embassy to the United States of America* (Tokyo: Foreign Affairs Association of Japan, 1958). Fukuzawa Yukichi's story can be followed in memoirs he dictated in old age and translated by Eiichi Kiyooka as *The Autobiography of Fukuzawa Yukichi* (Tokyo, Hokuseido, and New York, Columbia University Press Editions), and he is the subject of Carmen

Blacker's *The Japanese Enlightenment: A Study of the Writings of Fukuzawa Yukichi* (Cambridge: At the University Press, 1964). His *Gakumon no susume* has been translated by David Dilworth and Umeyo Hirano as *An Encouragement of Learning* (Tokyo: Sophia University, 1969).

The Iwakura mission is the subject of a forthcoming study by Marlene J. Mayo, who has already published valuable studies in "Rationality in the Restoration: The Iwakura Embassy," in Bernard S. Silberman and Harry D. Harootunian, eds., *Modern Japanese Leadership* (University of Arizona Press, 1966), and especially "The Western Education of Kume Kunitake, 1871-1876," *Monumenta Nipponica*, xxviii, 1 (Tokyo: Sophia University, 1973). Eugene Soviak also analyzes Kume's journal in "On the Nature of Western Progress: The Journal of the Iwakura Embassy," in Donald H. Shively, ed., *Tradition and Modernization in Japanese Culture* (Princeton: Princeton University Press, 1971). Kume's famous account is in the five-volume *Tokumei zenken taishi Bei-Ō kairan jikki* (A True Account of the Tour of the Special Embassy to America and Europe) (Tokyo, 1878, and recently republished with notes by Tanaka Akira from Iwanami, Tokyo, 1977). Professor Tanaka has also published *Iwakura shisetsudan* (Tokyo, 1977), and he has analyzed the mission's stay in the United States in "Iwakura shisetsutai no Amerika kan" (The Iwakura Party's View of America), in *Meiji kokka no tenkai to minshū seikatsu* (Turning Points in the Meiji State and People's Lives) (Tokyo: Kōbundo, 1975). Katō Shūichi treats the embassy in *Nihonjin no sekaizō*

(The Japanese World View), in *Kindai Nihon shisōshi kōza* (Lectures on Modern Japanese Thought) (Tokyo: Chikuma Shobo, 1961). Kume's memoirs, edited by Nakano Reishirō, appeared in 1934 as *Kume Hakushi kujūnen kaikoroku* (Tokyo, 2 vols.). Professor Haga treats the irony of Kume's career in a sensitive study, "Meiji shoki ichi chishikijin no seiyō taiken (The Western experience of an early Meiji intellectual)," in *Shimada Kinji Kyōju kanreki kinen rombunshū: Hikaku bungaku hikaku bunka* (Comparative Literature and Comparative Culture: Essays for the Sixtieth Birthday of Professor Shimada Kenji (Tokyo: Kobundo, 1961). I have discussed Meiji views of China and the West in "Changing Japanese Attitudes toward Modernization," in a conference volume edited by me under the same title (Princeton: Princeton University Press, 1965), and "Japanese Views of China during the Meiji Period," cited earlier. Naitō is studied by Yue-him Tam, "In Search of the Oriental Past: The Life and Thought of Naitō Konan (1866-1934)" (Princeton University dissertation, 1975), while Japanese study abroad has been studied by James T. Conte, "Overseas Study in the Meiji Period: Japanese Students in America, 1867-1902" (Princeton University dissertation, 1977).

The Twentieth Century

I have discussed the changing image of the imperial institution in "Monarchy and Modernization," *Journal of Asian Studies*, August 1977. Ishiwara Kanji is the subject of Mark Peattie's *Ishiwara Kanji and Japan's Confrontation with the West* (Princeton: Princeton University Press, 1975). Mr. Yoshida's recollections were translated by his son Yoshida Kenichi as *The Yoshida Memoirs* (Boston: Houghton Mifflin, 1962), and he is the subject of recent studies by J. W. Dower, *Empire and Aftermath: Yoshida Shigeru and the Japanese Experience, 1878-1954* (Cambridge: Harvard University Press, 1979) and Inoki Masamichi, *Hyōden Yoshida Shigeru* (Tokyo: Yomiuri, 3 vols., 1978-80). The minutes of the meetings that produced the decision for war have been translated by Nobutaka Ike as *Japan's Decision for War: Records of the 1941 Policy Conferences* (Stanford: Stanford University Press, 1967). Robert J. C. Butow, *Tōjō and the Coming of the War* (Princeton: Princeton University Press, 1961), adds much detail, and the problem of messages and misunderstandings is superbly treated by Roberta Wohlstetter, *Pearl Harbor: Warning and Decision* (Stanford: Stanford University Press, 1962). Admiral Nagano's summation of the case for war is cited by James Crowley in James Morley, ed., *Japan's Foreign Policy, 1868-1941: A Research Guide* (New York: Columbia University Press, 1957), p. 98. Dorothy Borg and Shumpei Okamoto, eds., *Pearl Harbor as History: Japanese-American Relations 1931-1941* (New York: Columbia University Press, 1973), provide parallel studies of American and Japanese groups influential in policy formation. The Matsumoto Shigeharu memoirs, originally published serially in *Rekishi to jimbutsu* (History and People), have appeared in book form as *Shanhai jidai* (The

Shanghai Era) (Tokyo: Chūō Kōron, 3 vols., 1974 and 1975 and in a single volume, 1977). Prince Saionji is quoted by Takashi Oka in "Saionji and the Manchurian Crisis," *Harvard Papers on China* (Harvard University: Committee on International and Regional Studies, 1954), p. 58. The point that Japan's postwar posture represents deliberate planning is developed by Martin E. Weinstein in *Japan's Postwar Defense Policy, 1947-1968* (New York: Columbia University Press, 1971), and Hata Ikuhiko in *Shiroku Nihon saigunbi* (History of Japan's Rearmament, Tokyo, 1976), and again in an as yet unpublished 1978 paper, "Origins of Japan's Post-war Rearmament" for the Conference on Security Arrangements in Northeast Asia, Harvard University, June 1978. Japan's possible standing as "Number One" is the theme of Ezra Vogel, *Japan as Number One: Lessons for America* (Cambridge: Harvard University Press, 1979). The literature on postwar Japanese political and economic developments grows constantly in volume and quality, but the most cogent overview is that of Edwin O. Reischauer, *The Japanese* (Cambridge: Harvard University Press, 1977).

INDEX